AMERICAN PRESIDENTS IN DIPLOMACY AND WAR

THOMAS R. PARKER

AMERICAN PRESIDENTS IN DIPLOMACY AND WAR

STATECRAFT, FOREIGN POLICY, AND LEADERSHIP

University of Notre Dame Press
Notre Dame, Indiana

University of Notre Dame Press
Notre Dame, Indiana 46556
undpress.nd.edu

All Rights Reserved

Copyright © 2023 by the University of Notre Dame

Published in the United States of America

Library of Congress Control Number: 2023937776

ISBN: 978-0-268-20723-6 (Hardback)
ISBN: 978-0-268-20725-0 (WebPDF)
ISBN: 978-0-268-20722-9 (Epub)

With gratitude to my family and close friends,
who taught me things more important than power politics.

CONTENTS

This book hopes to stimulate thinking about what makes for effective statecraft through a discussion of some of America's iconic presidents, as well as more recent presidents. The goal is to better understand why they were successful or not. Some of the chapters provide an overview of their entire diplomacy, notably that of George Washington, Abraham Lincoln, and Theodore Roosevelt. To provide focus, the chapter on Franklin Roosevelt concentrates on his diplomacy and presidential leadership leading up to the U.S. entry into World War II and the chapter on Harry Truman analyzes his administration's blunder into provoking Chinese intervention in Korea. There is a wide range of successes and failures to choose from in any period, of course, but the author feels that President Nixon's Middle East diplomacy and President George H. W. Bush's first Gulf War stewardship provide useful lessons about effective statecraft. Conversely, Presidents Carter and Obama, despite their international accomplishments, were tentative and uncertain about military power and diplomacy dealing with security issues. The author also discusses briefly, in the context of diplomatic relations with President Roosevelt, Prime Minister Winston Churchill's audacious decision to bomb the French fleet in 1940 to keep it out of German hands. Conversely, Churchill's prudent decision to avoid committing British troops to Vietnam in the 1950s demonstrates that restraint is as important as assertiveness in diplomacy and war. Such studies of history provide perspectives for students and practitioners of international relations to increase the prospects for success and to avoid being swept up by the passions of the moment.

ACKNOWLEDGMENTS

I want to thank several colleagues for their advice on this book. Each time they read the manuscript, it meant more work but a better result. They include the following:

Professor Denver Brunsman, George Washington University's leading scholar on the American Revolution and the early Federal period

Professor Klaus Larres of North Carolina University, noted historian of the Cold War period in Europe

Dr. Alan Makovsky, senior fellow at the Center for American Progress and one of the leading U.S. experts on Turkey and the Middle East

Dr. David Nickles, senior historian at the Office of the Historian at the Department of State

Professor Yafeng Xia, senior professor at Long Island University and a leading scholar on the Cold War in Asia

Dr. David Pollock, senior fellow at the Washington Institute for Near East Policy

I also wish to thank Kellie M. Hultgren and University of Notre Dame Press for their superb assistance.

INTRODUCTION

In 1953 an American exchange student asked Winston Churchill how one might prepare to meet the challenges of leadership. Churchill replied, "Study history. Study history."[1] To this end, this book is about the statecraft of selected American presidents, as defined by their exercise of diplomatic, military, and economic power. Its goal is to gain insights into why certain presidents were successful in statecraft and why others were less so.

We will devote chapters to the diplomacy and wartime leadership of America's most iconic leaders: Presidents George Washington, Abraham Lincoln, Theodore Roosevelt, and Franklin Roosevelt. In doing so, we will compare them to some of their illustrious but less successful contemporaries, notably Presidents Thomas Jefferson, James Madison, and Woodrow Wilson.

Statecraft requires the understanding of complex situations, the prudent evaluation of various courses of action, and the ability to learn, adapt, and anticipate, as well as determination. George Washington and his closest adviser, Alexander Hamilton, demonstrated these characteristics, as we will show in chapter 2. During the Revolutionary War, Washington learned from his initial battlefield defeats and adopted a more effective military strategy. Washington and Hamilton used the complicated European balance of power to their own purposes, first siding with France in the 1780s and then remaining neutral in the war between France and England in the 1790s. In contrast, Jefferson and Madison, who championed a more idealistic foreign policy based on solidarity among republics, stumbled into the War of 1812 when they failed to understand the balance of power among England, the United States, and Napoleon's France.

Statecraft, as discussed in chapter 3, may require the ability to combine aggressiveness with caution. President Abraham Lincoln did this when he acted prudently toward Britain and France, both of which supported the Southern cause, while prosecuting a relentless war against the southern states.

As mentioned, successful leaders have the ability to learn, including from their own mistakes. We will see in chapter 4 that, as assistant secretary of the navy, Theodore Roosevelt displayed an initial impulsive nationalism, advocating taking the Philippines from Spain in 1898 without understanding the difficulty of defending the islands from a rising Japan. As president, however, Roosevelt successfully mediated among the European and Asian powers while making America a naval world power for the first time. After World War I, Roosevelt and his close associate, Senator Henry Cabot Lodge, advocated for a political-military partnership with Britain and France, as opposed to Woodrow Wilson's more idealistic but less practical League of Nations, with its emphasis on deterring aggression through international public opinion.

Franklin Roosevelt's policy toward Europe before the entry of the United States into World War II epitomizes the diplomacy of guile, a sometimes-useful element of statecraft. As shown in chapter 5, Roosevelt led a dovish American public slowly toward possible participation in World War II. His policy was secretive, devious—and relentless. During the war he had no compunctions about making moral compromises to further the military effort.

Beginning with chapter 6, we examine historical cases from the post–World War II era. President Harry Truman, with his policy during the Korean War, is an example of a reasonable political leader who made serious mistakes in implementing otherwise well-founded policy, the defense of South Korea. Truman and his distinguished secretary of state, Dean Acheson, were swept along in the triumphalism of General Douglas MacArthur's bid to unite the entire Korean peninsula after his dramatic military success at Inchon in September 1950. Truman could have avoided the ensuing disaster of Chinese intervention if he had listened to the advice of the more prudent State Department adviser George Kennan.

In chapter 7 we see the importance of adapting to changing circumstances, as displayed by President Richard Nixon and Secretary of State Henry Kissinger during the 1973 Arab-Israeli War. Nixon and Kissinger first sent arms to Israel to avoid further Israeli military setbacks and then saved the Egyptian army once the war turned in favor of Israel. The post-war negotiations under Kissinger between Israel and the Arabs also provide lessons on challenging international negotiations.

Statecraft may involve the tensions inherent in difficult moral dilemmas and the need to stand up to public pressure. In chapter 8 we examine the debate within the Carter administration in 1978 about whether to urge the shah of Iran to crack down on Iranian protesters. Ignoring the advice of his national security adviser, Zbigniew Brzezinski, President Carter held back from doing so, only to blunder subsequently into an unrealistic attempt to liberate U.S. diplomatic personnel in Tehran. Careening from caution to recklessness, Carter also represented a turning point in U.S. foreign policy, initiating a new era in American politics in which candidates with no foreign policy experience became the norm for the first time since the 1920s.

President George H. W. Bush, an exception to this new norm, displayed a surer touch in his diplomacy and wartime leadership during the first Gulf War in 1990 and 1991. He did not flinch when his military advisers told him that he would have to commit most of the U.S. military to expelling Iraq from Kuwait, as we see in chapter 9. A subtle student of international affairs, Bush also embodied determination in successful statecraft.

Finally, in chapter 10, we examine the costs of inexperience and ambivalence toward military power. President Barack Obama brushed off the advice of his more seasoned advisers, who argued for prudence during the explosion of political unrest in the Arab world in 2011. He then stumbled into a counterproductive war in Libya. Wavering between imprudence and excessive caution, he subsequently rejected his advisers' advocacy of a firm response to Syrian president Bashar al-Assad's use of chemical weapons against his own citizens in 2013. Obama's secretary of defense, Ash Carter, felt that the president was displaying the naiveté and arrogance of a smart but inexperienced leader.

All of these case studies attempt to shed light on what makes for successful statecraft by studying the past to help guide the present and the future. An old adage says history does not repeat itself, but it does rhyme. Indeed, Churchill's advice to the student in 1953 also included the following: "In history lie all the secrets of statecraft."[2]

CHAPTER 1

What Makes for Successful Statecraft?

Before we turn to historical cases in detail, it would be useful to examine the main components of effective statecraft and provide some brief examples of successes and failures from U.S. and international history. Effective policy begins with understanding complex situations and their broad diplomatic, military, and economic aspects, including the motivations of other countries and their leaders, the stakes involved for one's own country, and public opinion.

The Vietnam War provides a useful example of a failure by successive leaders to understand a complex situation. The origins of the war went back to 1947, when President Truman rallied American public support for military and economic aid to Greece and Turkey and, by extension, to any country threatened by communist outside pressures. This position was buttressed by the famous *Foreign Affairs* article the same year on containment, "The Sources of Soviet Conduct," by U.S. diplomat George Kennan, who argued that Washington should oppose Soviet expansion. These were laudable as general principles, but as the journalist Walter Lippmann pointed out, the sweeping containment policy risked overcommitting the United States to defending weak regimes where Washington was at a comparative disadvantage. Moreover, Kennan himself qualified the implementation of the containment doctrine by saying that he had never meant that U.S. assistance always required a military component. In short, distinctions needed to be made.

Indeed, there were many reasons to be skeptical about the prospects for U.S. success in South Vietnam. Prime Minister Winston Churchill turned aside a U.S. request to help France in Indochina in 1954 and warned U.S. officials of "war on the fringes, where the Russians were strong [because they could offer assistance and sanctuary to the North Vietnamese] and could mobilize the enthusiasm of nationalist and oppressed peoples."[1] Churchill thought it best to defend Southeast Asia at the borders of Malaya (as Britain successfully did in its counterinsurgency campaign in the 1950s). The United States would help Thailand to defend itself in the 1960s.

There were other reasons to avoid intervention, in addition to Churchill's warnings about nationalism and the proximity of North Vietnam to Russia and China. Vietnam's terrain, with its lush vegetation, favored the Vietcong insurgents and worked against U.S. conventional forces with their dependence on airpower and artillery. The communist regime also mobilized the entire population of North Vietnam and the Vietcong guerrillas in South Vietnam. U.S. policymakers also failed to learn from France's military defeats in Vietnam in the 1950s. Overconfident U.S. leaders failed to discuss at length either these comparative disadvantages or the history of the intervention by the French.[2]

Finally, Professor Hans Morgenthau of the University of Chicago, one of the pioneering commentators on realism and foreign policy in the mid-twentieth century, went further by pointing out that the stakes were not that important in South Vietnam. After all, a united communist Vietnam would remain independent of China, given the historical rivalry between the two countries. Indeed, China and Vietnam engaged in a border war within several years of unification in the 1970s, and Vietnam remains an important partner of the United States in the loose coalition of East Asian countries opposed to Chinese expansion.[3]

Nor did U.S. policymakers step back from the discussion about a South Vietnam commitment to evaluate the bigger picture of America's comparative position in the Cold War rivalry. A more nuanced assessment might have gone along the following lines: the long struggle between the non-communist and communist worlds would probably involve some losses by both sides. Cuba, for example, would become a Soviet gain and Yugoslavia a Soviet loss during the early Cold War period. Overall, however, the U.S. position was reasonably solid, given the strong desire of many countries to avoid Soviet domination, including even communist China. One Cold War joke, for example, asked, Which is the only country surrounded by hostile communist states? The answer: the Soviet Union. Given the relatively strong geopolitical position of the United States and the internal weaknesses of the Soviet Union, the U.S. could afford to lose a country such as South Vietnam if the prospects for successful intervention at a reasonable cost were poor.

In short, U.S. leaders failed to come to grips with the many reasons why the commitment to support South Vietnam was not vital and would probably turn out poorly.

The Importance of Prudence

The eighteenth-century British parliamentarian Edmund Burke called prudence "the god of this lower world."[4] Prudence takes the understanding of complexity and relates it to actual policy decisions about what the United States might or might not do. What are the pros and cons of the various policy options? Their chances of success? What might be the costs if a given policy is successful? What are the various policy traps that should be avoided?

Prudent policy-making depends on the ability to examine and implement policy options as objectively and dispassionately as possible and to minimize wishful thinking, willfulness, and risk aversion. Abraham Lincoln, for example, was deliberative in his approach to political and military options.[5] According to Charles Dana, Lincoln's assistant, the president "had not freakish notions that things were so, or might be so, when they were not so. All this thinking and reasoning, all his mind, in short, was based continually upon actual facts, and upon facts which, as I said, he saw the essence."[6] Lincoln knew there were too many imponderables to forecast the outcomes of battles, and he never assumed that the North would win the Civil War. He was certain, however, that it would lose if it followed the strategy of General George McClellan, who was excessively fearful about engaging with Lee's army. Lincoln therefore made a bold move in removing McClellan despite the general's popularity with Union troops.

McClellan's risk-averse mentality is not rare among military and political leaders. In the first Gulf War, when U.S. military planners—most of whom were initially opposed to using military force—provided President George H. W. Bush with an unenthusiastic briefing about their cautious war plans, Deputy National Security Adviser Robert Gates said it reminded him of McClellan.[7] Bush did not remove those military planners, but he did tell them to come back with a more aggressive plan. Conversely, political leaders sometimes fall prey to the wishful thinking born of overconfidence. Their attitude usually reflects some combination of their natural optimism, the impact of recent successes, and the political temper of their time. President George W. Bush fell into this trap regarding Afghanistan and Iraq in the early 2000s.

Another dimension of prudence is the imperative to match means, the appropriate ways of applying them, and ends. Lippmann expressed this with his well-known formulation: "Without the controlling principles that the nation must maintain its objectives and its power in equilibrium, its purposes within its means and its means equal to its purposes, its commitments related to its resources and its recourses to its commitments, it is impossible to think at all about foreign affairs."[8]

President Franklin Roosevelt illustrated this judicious approach when he rejected the advice of his senior military leaders to consider invading France in 1942 and 1943. Instead, he accepted Churchill's counsel to postpone an invasion of France until the Allies had gained aerial and maritime superiority over Germany, as they did by 1944. Roosevelt and Churchill agreed to fight in the less demanding theater of North Africa and Sicily until then.

Roosevelt's policy leading up to World War II also demonstrates that guile sometimes has its place in statecraft, although U.S. politicians and the general public have generally frowned on its use. American diplomats, for example, stormed out of Paris in 1798 when French foreign minister Maurice de Talleyrand asked for a bribe before discussing their concerns about French harassment of American shipping in the XYZ Affair. Likewise, few U.S. political figures would make Henry Kissinger's reported joke about circumventing the congressionally mandated arms embargo against Turkey for its invasion of Cyprus in 1974: "The illegal we do immediately. The unconstitutional takes a little longer."[9]

Yet guile has its place in diplomacy and war. Churchill wrote that in wartime truth is so precious that it should be attended by a bodyguard of lies. Similarly, Franklin Roosevelt said, "I am perfectly willing to mislead and tell untruths [to the public], if it will help win the war."[10]

Moreover, guile does not always mean deceit. It can simply involve cunning. Lincoln, for example, outmaneuvered his opponents at the beginning of the American Civil War at the Union Fort Sumter in Charleston, South Carolina. The fort was running out of supplies soon after Lincoln took office, and most of his cabinet members recommended withdrawing U.S. forces before they were forced to capitulate. Lincoln, however, saw the dire situation as an opportunity to induce the South to fire the first shots of the Civil War. He informed Confederate leaders, therefore, that Washington would resupply the fort with provisions but no additional personnel or arms. This threat of no more personnel was meant to appeal to the states where slavery was legal, notably Kentucky and Maryland, but which were considering staying in the Union. The spirited but doomed defense of the fort was designed to appeal to the North. The southerners fell into the trap of firing first, and northerners volunteered for military service by the thousands.[11]

One of the most remarkable examples of deception in diplomacy involved Talleyrand's attempts to head off Napoleon's disastrous invasion of Russia. When the French emperor met Russian emperor Alexander I in 1808, Talleyrand decided to meet secretly with the tsar. First, Talleyrand would recommend to Napoleon what to say to the tsar. Talleyrand would then meet Alexander in secret to tell him what Napoleon was going to say and suggest to the tsar what he should say to Napoleon in return. It was a tour de force of deceit that many in France considered treasonous, but it was for a just cause.[12]

Groupthink

In addition to avoiding excessive caution or overconfidence, a prudent political leader should be aware of other dangerous traps. Students of statecraft have often been warned about the dangers of groupthink, when the dynamics of group cohesion discourage a thorough airing of various options. Historians have criticized President John F.

Kennedy for approaching the Bay of Pigs invasion of Cuba with this mindset, in contrast to his thoughtful handling of the Cuban missile crisis, during which he sought out various points of view.[13]

The Role of Public Opinion and the Political Ambiance

Any foreign policy must have some basic level of support from public opinion, or at least acquiescence, for it to succeed long term. At best, a committed president can go against public opinion if the price and risk are not too high. President Ronald Reagan, for example, went against the prevailing isolationist mood when he supported the Salvadoran government with U.S. trainers against a communist insurgency in the 1980s. As we shall see with Franklin Roosevelt, true intentions can also be disguised until the national mood changes in light of new circumstances.

At the same time, leaders must avoid the mistake of pursuing foolish policies to placate public opinion; at some point they are likely to pay a price. Despite his skepticism, President Kennedy approved the Bay of Pigs invasion of Cuba for fear of Republican criticism for not taking action against Cuban leader Fidel Castro.

Political leaders must also try to avoid being swayed by the ambient political atmosphere, often in reaction to the most recent international events, be they positive or negative. George W. Bush and most of his senior advisers were overly influenced by the relatively easy military victories in Kuwait and the Balkans in the 1990s and the initial success in Afghanistan in 2001. Iraq would be the same, they thought—incorrectly. In contrast, Presidents Carter and Obama, as we shall see, tended to act with excessive caution during security challenges in part because of the failure of the Vietnam War and the difficult conflicts in Afghanistan and Iraq.

The Slippery Slope or Mission Creep

Prudence requires an awareness of the dangers of how commitments can slide from modest engagements to unintended and overly ambitious ones. President Reagan began what he considered a modest U.S. troop commitment in Lebanon in 1982 to escort the Palestine Liberation Front's combatants out of Beirut in order to end the Israeli siege there. Once that was accomplished, he withdrew U.S. troops only to send them back to protect Palestinian civilians after massacres at several refugee camps. This mission then morphed into a more ambitious commitment to side with the Lebanese government against Hezbollah, the radical Shia organization. Hezbollah suicide bombers inflicted hundreds of casualties on several U.S. Marine barracks, thereby driving the United States out of Lebanon. Iraqi president Saddam Hussein drew the lesson that Americans would not tolerate casualties as part of his calculation in invading Kuwait in 1990. The U.S. setback in Somalia in the early 1990s went through a somewhat similar evolution from a modest initial commitment to a more ambitious and risky one.[14]

The Dangers of the Cautious Middle Path

While prudence avoids unnecessary risk, this does not mean that a prudent leader should always seek a cautious middle path that splits the difference between options. Such a path sometimes appears superficially appealing but can cause leaders to avoid tough but necessary decisions. When, for example, Italian dictator Benito Mussolini invaded Ethiopia in 1935, British and French leaders faced a dilemma. On the one hand, they could have opted for a forceful military move, such as closing the Suez Canal to Italy. On the other hand, Mussolini was still wary of Hitler's expansionist plans in the mid-1930s and the British and the French might have acquiesced to Italy's invasion in an attempt to form an anti-German front. Instead, Britain and the League of Nations agreed on a halfhearted international oil embargo against Italy. This created an impression of weakness while pushing Italy into an alliance with Germany. Better to have either responded forcefully, as Churchill advised when he was a member of Parliament, or accept the invasion, as the French government privately counseled. The middle path failed on all accounts.

Losing Interest in Policies

President Joseph Biden's withdrawal from Afghanistan in 2021 provides an excellent example of this danger. Reasonable observers could have differed over the president's decision to withdraw all U.S.

military forces in the spring of 2021 to end the trickle of casualties and to focus on other foreign policy priorities. However, once he made the decision to withdraw, he and his senior advisers lost their focus on the country. U.S. military commanders reasoned that if the president was uninterested, they might as well leave Afghanistan as quickly as possible to minimize military casualties. Thus, U.S. military forces withdrew before the total withdrawal of U.S. citizens and friendly Afghans, thereby causing the notorious chaos at the Kabul airport and the decision to send back U.S. military forces. Ironically, the early withdrawal may have resulted in more military casualties than would have been the case if the military had remained until all civilians were evacuated. Thoughtful leaders therefore must monitor important commitments even as they are being brought to an end.[15]

Failure of Imagination

Political leaders may stumble badly when they fail to consider all relevant policy options. For example, after Osama bin Laden and al-Qaeda attacked U.S. embassies in East Africa in 1998, the Clinton administration debated whether to respond with cruise-missile attacks lasting only several hours against the al-Qaeda camps or whether to attack them periodically. No one considered focusing the response against al-Qaeda's Taliban hosts. Cruise-missile attacks were never going to dissuade Bin Laden from attacking U.S. targets. But the Taliban had something to lose, and U.S. leaders could have told them either to stop Bin Laden from attacking U.S. targets or be prepared to see much of Afghanistan's infrastructure destroyed. To drive home the point, the U.S. could have destroyed a target such as the Kandahar airport, striking at night to avoid civilian casualties.[16]

Another missed opportunity to debate all relevant options occurred when the George W. Bush administration failed to consider the possibility of conducting periodic air strikes on suspected Iraqi nuclear and biological weapons facilities instead of a large ground invasion. A careful evaluation of this option might have concluded that any nuclear program probably could be contained through airstrikes, given the large scope of such programs. Since biological programs are smaller and easier to hide, a decision to launch a ground invasion may have come down to the scope of the biological weapons threat. Reasonable advisers might have differed over the best response, but the option of air strikes was never considered because the administration was carried away by the sense of vulnerability after the 9/11 attacks and by hubris after the early success against the Taliban in Afghanistan.

George W. Bush and Obama, along with most of their advisers, also failed to consider the full array of policy options regarding Afghanistan. Both tried to gain control over the entire country (U.S. troops reached their peak at about one hundred thousand under Obama), which in fact comprised several very different regions. The Turkic and Tajik/Iranian peoples in northern and western Afghanistan were largely opposed to the Taliban. In contrast, the Pashtun peoples of southern and eastern Afghanistan were friendlier to the Taliban, who could take advantage of mountainous terrain and sanctuaries in Pakistan. Neither Bush nor Obama considered focusing the U.S. military effort on securing military bases around Kabul and in the north and west rather than in the entire country. These would have served as bases to search for and attack al-Qaeda and Bin Laden in Pakistan. Vice President Biden was the only voice advocating for something along these lines during the Obama administration.[17]

Another form of a failure of imagination relates to the advice that senior foreign policy advisers provide to the president. Advisers discuss and debate policies among themselves and seek to do so in a coolly detached and analytical manner. However, they should remember that a president must explain and defend the policy before the nation and the world. For example, before the North Korean invasion of South Korea in 1950, President Truman's military advisers advocated abandoning South Korea. They failed to imagine how Truman might respond to an actual invasion. Understanding one's own side is as important as understanding the adversary.

To summarize, prudent action requires a rigorous weighing of all the pros and cons of various courses of action before a policy commitment is decided upon and implemented as well as an awareness of the range of policy traps. As Hans Morgenthau wrote, "Realism, then, considers prudence—the weighing of the consequences of alternative political actions—to be the supreme virtue in politics."[18]

The Realm of Action: The Imperative of Determination

Once policies are decided upon, particularly those involving military force, understanding complexity and exercising prudence remain essential, but other characteristics of statecraft also come into play. If prudence dominates intelligent policy discussions about various courses of action, determination is needed to implement decisions unwaveringly. Determination does not guarantee success, but its absence will result in failure.

As Secretary of State Kissinger wrote about the successful threat of intervention by U.S. and Israeli military forces to force the Syrian army to withdraw from northern Jordan, which it had invaded in the 1970s, "A leader must choose carefully and thoughtfully, the issues over which to face confrontation. He should do so only for major objectives. Once he is committed, however, his obligation is to end the confrontation rapidly. For this he must convey implacability."[19] More concisely, Napoleon reportedly said, "If you begin to take Vienna, take Vienna."

The first Israeli prime minister, David Ben-Gurion, conveyed implacability. With the outbreak of the first Arab-Israeli War in May 1948, all four Jewish militia forces pledged to merge into one organization, the Israeli Defense Forces. However, the mainstream Haganah and its Palmach units remained rivals with the smaller and more militant Irgun Zvai Leumi (IZL), headed by Menachem Begin. In June 1948 the IZL organized a large shipment of arms and men from Europe to Israel on the *Altalena* with the intention of keeping most, if not all, of the arms for its own forces. Ben-Gurion insisted that all the arms be sent to the new, centralized Israeli Defense Forces command and ordered Palmach units under the command of Yitzhak Rabin to open fire on the ship as it approached Tel Aviv, resulting in the deaths of eighteen IZL combatants. Ben-Gurion later said that when the Jews finally built the Third Temple (the first and second having been destroyed by the Babylonians and Romans respectively), the "holy cannon" that sank the *Altalena* would find its place at the side of the altar.[20]

Perhaps the most striking example of audacity was Churchill's decision to bomb the French fleet in North Africa in July 1940. Once Germany and France had signed an armistice ending hostilities, Churchill dreaded that Berlin would force Paris into turning over its navy to Germany. He pleaded with the French to unite their naval forces with the British navy, send them to the French West Indies, or sabotage them. When the French refused, Churchill ordered a naval and air attack on the French fleet in North Africa that killed over a thousand French sailors. We will study further this example from British history of implacable determination in our chapter on President Franklin Roosevelt.[21]

Combining Intellect with Action: The Need to Learn, to Adapt, and to Anticipate

Along with single-minded focus, effective statecraft also requires the ability to learn, to adapt, and to anticipate. As noted, George Washington and Theodore Roosevelt learned from early mistakes and Secretary of State Henry Kissinger adapted U.S. policy to changing circumstances during the 1973 Arab-Israeli War. On the other hand, we shall see that during the wars between Britain and France Thomas Jefferson and James Madison failed to anticipate the counterproductive dangers of their own aggressive policies against British maritime harassment.

Adapting to changing circumstances involves grappling with the complexity of new realities. Many observers thought the invasion of Iraq in 2003 was a mistake. However, once it began, a strong case could also be made for seeing it through, as President George W. Bush did in making his unpopular but successful 2006 decision to send additional troops to Iraq. Similarly, President Obama's opposition to the Iraq War while he was a U.S. senator may have been justified, but his withdrawal of all U.S. forces from Iraq in 2012 contributed to the rise of the Islamic State.

Similarly, President Dwight Eisenhower may have been right to oppose British and French military intervention in Egypt in 1956. However, it was arguably a mistake to force Britain and France to desist once the war started because Egyptian president Gamal Abdel Nasser would go on to claim falsely that he had defeated the British and French in battle. The Egyptian people fell for the ruse, and an emboldened Nasser blundered into a disastrous defeat by Israel in 1967.[22]

Adaptability also requires sometimes reconsidering one's partners and one's adversaries. Perhaps the United States should have considered supporting the secular communist government of Najibullah in Kabul once the Soviets withdrew from Afghanistan in 1989. While pro-Soviet, he would have been less of a threat than the Taliban, which Pakistan helped put in power in 1996.

Finally, leaders must acknowledge when their policies are not succeeding and adapt to reality. Presidents Reagan and Clinton pulled out of Lebanon and Somalia respectively without too much agonizing because U.S. interests were relatively limited and U.S. losses were modest in number. In contrast, President Nixon and Secretary of State Kissinger pursued the prospects of an independent South Vietnam over four years in the hopes of defending national credibility and avoiding the depredations of victorious communist movements, such as the Cambodian mass exterminations. However, preventing communist victories was unlikely, given declining American domestic support and North Vietnam's determination and support from China and Russia. Moreover, the longer the United States stayed in South Vietnam, the stronger the anti-intervention reaction of the U.S. public. American troops arguably should have withdrawn more quickly but still in an orderly fashion. Thus in statecraft even determination, the twin brother of prudence, must recognize its limits.

Interests and Ideals

Prudent leaders have tended to be wary of moralism in foreign policy and have been willing to make moral compromises for larger purposes. Franklin Roosevelt summed up his approach to foreign policy with a Balkan proverb: "My children, you are permitted in time of great danger to walk with the Devil until you have crossed the bridge." So he told the press privately to justify working with morally compromised individuals in the French Vichy government to help the World War II effort in North Africa.[23]

Prudent leaders also tend to avoid making the promotion of democracy a major feature of foreign policy for several reasons. Stable democracies usually require a minimum economic and social foundation; in their absence, authoritarian leaders can use unstable conditions to take power through ostensibly democratic elections, as evidenced by Hitler in the 1930s, Venezuelan president Hugo Chávez in 1999, Hamas in the Gaza Strip in 2007, and the Muslim Brotherhood in Egypt in 2013. Sometimes there are also trade-offs regarding unstable democracies: the democratic regime that emerged briefly in Tunisia after the Arab protest movements in 2011 was less able to control terrorism than its autocratic predecessor.

Moreover, supporting democratic movements requires an involvement in the internal affairs of countries that may create its own problems. As laudable as U.S. attempts have been to support democratic forces in Russia, they probably contributed to President Vladimir Putin's decision to disrupt the 2016 U.S. election and may actually have hurt the opposition movement inside Russia, given the general antipathy to the United States there. Similarly, the U.S. government's high-profile support for anti-Russian political forces in Ukraine during the Bush and Obama administrations probably factored into Putin's decision to invade Ukraine in 2014 and 2022.

Prudent leaders should also be wary of humanitarian intervention. The United States has limited military and political capital to spend internationally, and it should be saved for major challenges to U.S. interests. Moreover, humanitarian intervention often proves ineffective because the U.S. public is not willing to support sustained intervention if no visible interests are at stake, as was the case in Lebanon in the early 1980s. Similarly, Kissinger warned about the dangers of the slippery slope in Somalia in the early 1990s before American and other foreign troops were murdered and mutilated. He foresaw that Washington would work with some armed groups, thereby alienating others, as occurred when the warlord Muhammad Aydid turned against international forces.[24]

Finally, not all cultures share the Western enthusiasm for pluralism and democratic elections, at least for the time being. Most rural Chinese seem to prefer autocrats and strongmen to democratic pluralism; a similar dynamic appears to be at play in the small towns and rural areas of Russia. Moreover, even when peoples of foreign countries find some elements of democracy and freedom attractive, nationalism and religious movements usually have stronger appeal by fostering a sense of belonging and sometimes rejection of the outside culture.[25]

Let us now turn to the foreign policies of some of America's most illustrious past presidents and some of its more recent ones. As Churchill counseled, under close analysis history can help educate political leaders and engaged citizens. And, as the nineteenth-century German chancellor Otto von Bismarck reportedly said, "A fool learns from his mistakes, a wise man learns from the mistakes of others."

CHAPTER 2

Washington, Hamilton, Jefferson, and Madison

The Diplomacy of Realism versus the Diplomacy of Ideology and Uncertainty

George Washington was not a warm, sentimental man. He was courteous but maintained a strong reserve. Once his colleague Gouverneur Morris bet his friends that he could gently place his arm on Washington's shoulder in a cheery greeting. Washington gave him a withering look, and Morris told his friends afterward it was the last time he, or anyone else, would do that.

Washington was hard on those who surrounded him. He once criticized Alexander Hamilton for being late for a meeting, leading Hamilton to submit his resignation, which Washington rejected. The president refused his officers' pleas to execute Major John André, who had been working with General Benedict Arnold to surrender the fort at West Point to the British, by a firing squad instead of hanging him as a common spy. While hard on others, he was also demanding of himself. He drove himself relentlessly during the Revolutionary Wars, never benefiting from better material conditions than his men, including during the miserable winter at Valley Forge. Although Washington had an explosive temper, his rage would pass and he would return to the subject under discussion. At times excessively sensitive to criticism, he never forgot slights but would not allow them to determine his actions.

Above all, Washington was a prudent man. Jefferson said it best: "Perhaps the strongest feature of his character was prudence, never acting until every circumstance, every consideration was maturely weighted; refraining if he saw a doubt, but, when decided, going through with his purpose whatever obstacles opposed."[1]

Hamilton, Washington's closest aide during the Revolutionary War and his presidency, complemented Washington well. Unlike Washington, Hamilton had sheer intellectual brilliance and a conceptual understanding of issues gained from his university training and extensive reading. At the same time, he could be high-handed and abrasive; unlike Washington, he made enemies. Hamilton once counseled Washington to warn Congress in so many words that the colonial army could force its hand about the payment of long-delayed salaries by marching toward Philadelphia; Washington rejected the proposal.

What united Washington and Hamilton more than anything, other than their dedication to American independence, was their belief in a pragmatic, clear-eyed foreign policy grounded in concrete U.S. interests. They engaged in objective, unsentimental analysis of those interests, particularly when the United States was threatened with being drawn into the wars of the French Revolution starting in the 1790s. Once they concluded that the alliance with France dating from the American Revolutionary War no longer served U.S. interests, they jettisoned it; interest, not sentiment, loyalty, or ideology, determined their policies. *Prudence* was their watchword, particularly since the American republic was still fragile. They understood the complexity of the predatory world of European power politics and considered Britain, France, and Spain to be potential threats, but also potential partners, depending upon changing circumstances.

In contrast, Thomas Jefferson and his close colleague James Madison favored a more idealist foreign policy based on solidarity among republics in the belief that this would usher in a new era of peace among nations. They believed that republican government fostered peace and prosperity because the average citizen wanted exactly that, whereas monarchies tended to drift toward war in part because European aristocracies justified their existence in that way. Jefferson and Madison were sympathetic to republican France's crusade against European monarchies in the 1790s and believed that

France and the United States represented a new phenomenon in world politics in which the interests and ideals of republican governments would coincide.

Behind these varying political worldviews lay different deep-seated psychological attitudes. Washington and Hamilton were comfortable using military and diplomatic power; they did not shy away from conflict whether on the battlefield or in political arenas. In contrast, Jefferson and Madison tended to be wary of the potential dangers of centralized political power. Jefferson even shied away from conflict in his personal life.

Domestic politics shaped the views of these leaders. Since the late 1600s, first in the Netherlands and then in England, urban banks, financial markets, and paper money had encroached on the power of the traditional landowning elite. Similar developments took place in the American colonies during the 1700s, a trend that Hamilton saw in New York City. While Washington came from agricultural Virginia, his experience as commander in chief had given him a national vision. In contrast, Jefferson and Madison regarded the growing urban economy in the northern and mid-Atlantic states with suspicion, and Jefferson went so far as to warn about subordinating agriculture to commerce. As a result, they opposed a professional army for fear that it might be used against the state of Virginia. They even turned against an oceangoing navy for fear that it would require heavy taxation, thereby strengthening the central government, and could draw the United States into foreign wars.

In short, Washington and Hamilton, followed by President John Adams, were the first test case in American history between two distinct approaches to foreign policy. Washington and Hamilton grounded their policies in concrete interest whereas Jefferson and Madison believed that national goals sprang from the idealism of republican solidarity.

Initially, however, Washington was neither realistic nor successful on the battlefield. As a general he demonstrated remarkable courage under fire, unrelenting physical stamina, and an absolute will to victory. However, while his indomitable drive was necessary for success, it could at times result in rigidity. During his first year as commander, Washington sought a set piece, a decisive battle of the sort that Napoleon would make famous, preferably a glorious assault on entrenched

British positions. He found the prospect of cowering in fortifications humiliating; worse yet would be guerrilla warfare. His favorite play, performed at his request at Valley Forge, was Joseph Addison's *Cato*, in which the proud Roman republican leader chooses suicide over submission to Caesar. Washington, like a modern-day Cato, planned to defeat the British in glorious battle or die trying.

During the summer of 1776 the British, with their better-trained military forces, took advantage of Washington's willful pride. They sent thirty thousand well-trained soldiers to crush Washington's twenty-thousand-man militia in Brooklyn and Manhattan. Washington refused the advice of his generals—including Nathanael Greene, who came to be one of his most trusted leaders—to adopt a guerrilla strategy of sharp, quick attacks on exposed British forces followed by withdrawals. Rather than a strategy of annihilation, Greene counseled Washington to adopt the Fabian approach, named after the Roman general Fabius who defeated Hannibal in Italy with guerrilla tactics, reasoning that it was the best option for the weaker side in just such a war.

Washington insisted, however, on fighting a conventional war, and, as a result, the British smashed the poorly trained American militia in Brooklyn Heights on August 29, 1776, less than two months after the Declaration of Independence. Greene reported that a listless Washington had to be led away to the last retreating boat to Manhattan: so "vexed" was he that "he sought death rather than life." Washington's senior military leaders subsequently voted ten to three to accept Greene's recommendation to abandon lower Manhattan: "Your Excellency had the choice of but two things, to fight the Enemy without the least Prospect of Success ... or remain inactive, & be the subject of Censure of an ignorant & impatient populace."[2] Washington refused the advice. The British then routed the Americans again in lower Manhattan, with Washington again being dragged from the battlefield by his own men. The British might have finished the war immediately if they had pursued the remnants of Washington's army more aggressively.

The debacle in New York forced Washington to put aside his rigid sense of honor in favor of a protracted guerrilla campaign, thereby subordinating his own ego for the good of the country. He subsequently avoided large-scale battles, with the exception of Brandywine in September 1777, when the congress decided that the colonial capital of Philadelphia could not be abandoned without a fight. He won skirmishes against minor British detachments at Princeton and Trenton and lost them at Germantown and Monmouth. He would return to conventional war only in 1781, when he combined his forces with French military forces to defeat a weakened Charles Cornwallis at Yorktown.

In short, Washington had learned about the need for flexibility, as well as determination, in wartime. Supreme acts of will were not enough to achieve success; he had to link determination with cunning.[3]

Washington's and Hamilton's Prudence in Diplomacy

Washington's ego was less at play in the more refined but equally deadly world of diplomacy. He pursued a realist policy that did not succumb to the passions of the moment, particularly over the budding American relationship with France, its former adversary from the Seven Years' War (1756–1763). Thus, when France entered into an alliance with the United States in 1778 after the American victory at Saratoga, Washington turned aside the proposal by the Marquis de Lafayette, whom he regarded as the son he had never had, to encourage the French to drive the British from Canada. In a letter to Henry Laurens, president of the Continental Congress, Washington wrote that foreign policy was driven by interests, not ideals: "Men are apt to run into extremes. . . . Hatred to England may carry some into excessive Confidence in France. . . . I am heartily disposed to entertain the most favorable sentiments of our new ally and to cherish them in others to a reasonable degree: but it is a maxim founded on the universal experience of mankind, that no nation is to be trusted farther than it is bound by its interest; and no prudent statesman or politician will venture to depart from it."[4]

The last thing Washington wanted was to have the new American states surrounded by the French to the north, their Spanish ally to the south and west, and the Native Americans in what is now Ohio, Indiana, and Illinois, with whom the French traditionally had had good relations. If the Americans could drive the British from Canada, fine, but he did not want them to be replaced by the French.

In fact, Washington was right about France's motives, though for the wrong reason. The French were less interested in the daunting task of retaking and holding Canada than in keeping the British there for two purposes. A British presence would make the Americans dependent on France for protection, and the American presence along the Eastern Seaboard would make Spain dependent on France for protection against the Americans. Therefore, the French went one better than Washington in the subtle, if devious, pursuit of their interests.[5]

Hamilton shared Washington's diplomatic analysis. While he would have preferred to be a military officer in the field, his staff position allowed him insights into the political intrigues of European rulers who saw the war as an opportunity to weaken Britain rather than to help the Americans. Hamilton also probably sensed the different agenda of the French military officers, with whom he could converse in French, including their favoring of the territorial interests of the Spanish over the Americans. These insights added to the understanding he had gained as a young man on the island of Nevis, observing the British, French, and Spanish promoting their competing interests in the Caribbean. All of this would prove to be good training for understanding the world of power politics that surrounded the new American republic.

The challenges facing Washington and Hamilton became more difficult several months after Washington's inauguration in March 1789. A mob of French artisans, wine merchants, and disaffected soldiers stormed the Bastille prison to liberate what they assumed were hundreds of political prisoners, but the mob only found four forgers, two psychotics, and one aristocrat. It was neither the first nor the last time that a revolutionary movement would act more viciously than the defenders of a rather ineffective regime.

The monarchy's subsequent fall in 1792 led to a series of wars between France and the traditional European monarchies, which threatened to drag the United States into the conflict between France and Britain. The British-French wars provoked a fierce debate in the United States about where American interests lay. Hamilton led those who favored a strict position of neutrality; Jefferson favored a neutrality that still tilted toward republican France, as did his close colleague James Madison, leader of the House of Representatives.

While Washington tried to mediate between the two factions, he largely shared Hamilton's views.

Jefferson and most fellow members of his Republican Party (later Democratic-Republican Party) strongly favored France because they thought that the new French republic would combine with the American republic to foster more republican governments throughout Europe and perhaps Latin America. As republics, he believed, they would be less inclined toward war because the average citizen wanted be left alone to pursue a quiet, comfortable, commercial life.

Hamilton disagreed. He believed that republican ideology would be less important than concrete national priorities and that American interests lay primarily with Britain in large part because it was by far the United States' major trading partner: 90 percent of U.S. imports came from Britain, and 50 percent of its exports went there. Moreover, neither Britain nor the United States wanted any aggressive European nation to create a powerful coalition that would unite all the European powers, as Louis XIV had attempted to do a century before. This could threaten a vulnerable America and even Britain. France had the potential to create such a coalition.

These varying views did not emerge immediately because nearly all Americans reacted with initial enthusiasm to the storming of the Bastille, recalling their own revolt against the British. Lafayette gave the key to the Bastille to Thomas Paine, who conveyed the memento to the new American president via John Rutledge Jr. Washington mounted it in his office, ironically along with a portrait of King Louis XVI.

Jefferson, still the U.S. envoy in Paris, expressed his usual sunny, optimistic views in letters to Washington after the fall of the Bastille, despite the mob's decapitation of several government officials and mutilation of the bodies. He made a joke to his friend Maria Cosway about checking to see if his head was still there in the morning because executions were frequent. More seriously, Jefferson advised moderation for all parties.

In October 1789 Hamilton was the first U.S. official to take a more somber view of the new revolution in France. He wrote to his old friend Lafayette, who had been appointed head of the French National Guard, "I have seen with a mixture of pleasure and apprehension the progress of the events which have lately taken place in your country. As a friend to mankind and liberty, I rejoice in the efforts which you are making to establish it, while I fear for the final success of the attempts, for the fate of those I esteem who are engaged in it."[6]

Political violence in France took a turn for the worse in June 1791 after Louis XVI was arrested while fleeing Paris to rally friendly French forces against the revolution and to save his life. Jefferson, now back in the United States, lamented that he had never seen Washington "so much dejected by any event in my life."[7] While Washington and Hamilton increasingly recoiled from the political violence in France, Jefferson's followers tended to dismiss these accounts as Federalist exaggerations. But Jefferson himself knew better because William Short, his deputy in Paris and a close friend, had stayed on after Jefferson's departure and warned him in a 1792 letter about "those mad and corrupted people in France who under the name of liberty have destroyed their own government." Jefferson replied to Short that while he regretted the loss of life, he still approved of the French Revolution because it had strengthened the new brotherhood of republics and hurt the Federalists politically: "The liberty of the whole earth was depending on the issue of the contest. . . . Rather than it should have failed, I would have seen half the earth desolated."[8] Jefferson was no doubt indulging in hyperbole, but the statement shows that he felt the revolution's bloody path would justify a coming age of pacific, democratic republican governments.

Nonetheless, in August 1792 Maximilien Robespierre and Jean-Paul Marat accelerated the executions; thousands of political opponents died by guillotine in addition to homeless people, prostitutes, and the inventor of the guillotine himself. Lafayette fled France for his life. Hamilton and Washington received reports about the mass killings from the new U.S. envoy to France, Gouverneur Morris. A mob almost lynched Morris before he convinced them that he was not British but an American who had lost his leg fighting alongside the French against the British; the crowd immediately hoisted him into the air as their hero. (In fact, he had lost his leg in a childhood accident.) Even the Jeffersonians could no longer dismiss the bloodbath as Federalist fake news.[9]

The debates in the American republic about the French Revolution gained a sense of urgency as the violence in France began to draw in other European powers. In August 1792, as the Terror gained momentum, France proclaimed itself a republic; in November it declared its willingness to assist all European peoples who wanted to overthrow their monarchical rulers and join the new republican crusade. Hamilton feared that this would result in a general European war. Jefferson, while concerned that the sweeping French declarations needlessly insulted European monarchs, still felt that the monarchs were mainly to blame for the hostilities and for opposing republican government.

In January 1793 French revolutionaries executed the king. According to his Irish confessor, Henry Essex Edgeworth, Louis XVI spoke with great dignity before his execution, pardoning those who had ordered it and wishing that the blood to be shed would never be visited on France. His severed head was thrust between his legs, and bits of his hair were sold for souvenirs.[10] The king's prayers would not be answered, as Britain and France declared war on each other in February 1793.

Both France and Britain were acting out of traditional foreign policy realism, as Washington and Hamilton had felt. Britain declared war on France less due to the king's execution and more because France had crossed London's red line against invading Belgium and Holland. Similarly, France seemed to vindicate Hamilton's realist writings in the *Federalist* no. 6, in which he wrote that all nations — including republics — may engage in war to achieve international domination (the implicit goals of revolutionary France), economic gain (France confiscated property and extracted taxes in Belgium and elsewhere), and their leaders' political advantage (French leaders thought that war would prove the death knell of the French monarchy and aristocracy).[11]

The United States was now faced with several concrete foreign policy decisions, not just general debates. Since its 1778 alliance treaty with France included a pledge to help defend French possessions in the Caribbean in return for French assistance during the Revolutionary War, the United States faced the prospect of being dragged into hostilities if France asked for support. Moreover, revolutionary France had brought Britain and Spain together in an anti-republican alliance despite their traditional rivalries; if Britain and Spain combined forces in North America, they could bottle up the still-vulnerable American republic and perhaps even destroy it.

Even if France did not ask for the activation of the 1778 alliance in the Caribbean, the United States had to decide whether it would maintain strict neutrality or favor its fellow republic. While most Americans, and certainly Jefferson and Madison, favored France over Britain, few wanted to intervene openly to help France. However, many advocated allowing French privateers to use U.S. ports—particularly those in southern states, the political base of Jefferson and Madison—to attack British commercial vessels.

In April 1793 the cabinet met to discuss U.S. policy toward the belligerents. Jefferson argued that America owed France a debt of gratitude that should be honored in some fashion. However, Hamilton dominated the cabinet debates in brilliant, lengthy disquisitions without notes on why strict neutrality served U.S. interests, referring to international law, relevant economic theory, lessons from Roman history, and particularly the European political scene. To Jefferson's dismay, Washington came down on Hamilton's side in favor of strict neutrality, including forbidding French privateers from using U.S. ports. Washington also decided that it was the executive branch that would determine U.S. foreign policy and not Congress, as Madison and Jefferson privately advocated.

However, the strict neutrality policy had to be sold to the public. In the summer of 1793, therefore, Hamilton in his "Pacificus" newspaper articles made the following arguments. Siding with France would be dangerous because it would expose the United States to attacks from the two other main North American powers, Britain and Spain, and their Native American allies. Siding with France would also be ineffective because the U.S. armed forces had limited capabilities. Moreover, France supported the Americans during the Revolutionary War for its own self-interested motive of reducing the power of its rival England, rather than from true idealism, and the 1778 treaty committed the United States to come to France's assistance in defensive wars, whereas France had initiated the current hostilities.

More broadly, Hamilton placed these arguments in a classical context of political realism regarding moral issues: "The rule of morality is ... not exactly the same between Nations as between individuals," including in feelings of gratitude.[12] That is, individuals could go out of their way to help others for a disinterested reason and could even subordinate their own interests in doing so. However, a nation's rulers must put their country's interests first because their decisions affect huge numbers of individuals.

Jefferson privately implored Madison to answer Hamilton's articles: "Cut him to pieces in the face of the public. There is nobody else who can and will enter the lists with him."[13] Madison initially demurred and only reluctantly agreed to answer Hamilton under the pseudonym "Helvidius." In more pedestrian prose, he argued for congressional primacy in foreign policy and accused Hamilton of being a British agent. These arguments fell flat. Hamilton had won the debate.[14]

While Hamilton had prevailed on policy, the war in Europe was not going to leave the American republic alone in its policy of neutrality. Britain began to expand its navy to blockade French ports and defeat the French navy in combat. To meet these goals, the Royal Navy began impressing sailors on U.S. and other foreign ships. This included British sailors who had left British ships to work on better-paid American merchant vessels and British immigrants to the United States, since London considered anyone born in Britain to be a British citizen. (By the end of the French-British wars in 1815, Britain had impressed around ten thousand sailors from U.S. vessels, some 7 to 9 percent of its entire navy.) Moreover, Britain also began seizing U.S. ships carrying French West Indian produce to France on the high seas, a trade the French had abandoned.

The George Washington of the early Revolutionary War might well have considered going to war over these violations of the nation's sovereignty. However, by this point, Washington, like Hamilton, believed that there were several reasons to seek some kind of accommodation with Britain short of war. First, the United States was not in a position to contest British naval superiority. The new republic had fewer than twenty oceangoing vessels; the British had six hundred. When a British warship ordered a U.S. merchant ship to stop at sea, there was not much of a choice. The military balance on the ground with Canada was less asymmetrical, but the United States had not had much success when it tried to take Montreal during the American Revolution.

Second, war would inflict major damage on the United States internally and perhaps tear it apart. Ending trade with Britain would have been a major blow to the American economy; half of its trade was with Britain, and customs revenues provided almost all government funding. New England was particularly dependent on trade with Britain and would be particularly opposed to war. In addition, while no American supported British interference with U.S. merchant vessels, the fact that the British were searching for their own former sailors may have taken some of the sting out of the impressment campaign.

Third, the United States did not have an interest in a French victory in Europe or over Britain, as even Jefferson conceded. A Europe united under French rule would probably result in an eventual French return to North America. In fact, Napoleon planned to do just this until his troops were defeated by Haitian insurgents and yellow fever in the early 1800s.

In contrast, as Hamilton wrote, Britain "repeatedly upheld the balance of power [in Europe], in opposition to the grasping power of France. She has no doubt occasionally employed the pretense of danger as the instrument of her own ambition; but it is not the less true, that she has been more than once an effectual shield against real danger."[15] Hamilton was presumably referring in part to Winston Churchill's ancestor the Duke of Marlborough, who had helped to defeat Louis XIV's grasp for French hegemony in Europe almost a century earlier.

Ultimately, Washington and Hamilton felt that the United States should bide its time for several decades until it was powerful enough to stand up to Britain or any combination of foreign powers. As Washington had learned on the battlefield during the first year of the American Revolution, sometimes one had to pursue a strategy of prudence over confrontation.

Nonetheless, Washington and the Federalists wanted to be prepared for war in the event of a worst-case scenario; at a minimum, a stronger navy would strengthen the U.S. bargaining position against the British. Washington therefore obtained funding to build six frigates; Hamilton organized contracts for naval munitions. Ironically, while the Democratic-Republicans called for a more confrontational policy toward Britain, they opposed increased defense spending because the necessary taxation and greater military capabilities would result in a stronger central government. If Federalists spoke softly, they still intended to carry a stick of some sort; the Republicans spoke loudly and shunned the stick. This would not be the last time the party of Jefferson and Madison would fail to back up their foreign policy with adequate military power.[16]

Jefferson resigned as secretary of state to return to Monticello in late 1793, partly because Washington generally sided with Hamilton and partly because Jefferson never had much stomach for the brass-knuckled world of American politics. His close friend and colleague James Madison became the leader of the Democratic-Republican Party. Under his leadership, in April 1794 the party passed a bill in the House, by a vote of fifty-four to forty-four, to prohibit all trade with Britain in protest against impressment. The Republicans, including Jefferson, touted this measure as an example of the new doctrine of "peaceful coercion" whereby commercial sanctions could bend Europe to the American will without having to resort to war. In contrast, Washington and the Federalists believed that peaceful coercion was wishful thinking, given that half of U.S. exports went to Britain and only one-sixth of British exports came to America.

Washington and the Federalists therefore decided to send an envoy to London to work out an understanding with Britain to avoid open warfare. Initially, Federalist congressional leaders wanted to send Hamilton, their champion, but he took himself out of consideration, feeling that he was too controversial a figure. In his letter of withdrawal, Hamilton advised Washington that even though the United States had an overwhelming interest in peace with Britain, war was still a danger, given the volatility of the situation: "Wars oftener proceed from angry and perverse emotions rather than from cool calculation of interest."[17] Hamilton may have been thinking of Republican political rallies, where imitation French guillotines were paraded about as warnings to the Federalists.

The Federalists then agreed on sending Chief Justice John Jay, who arrived in London in June 1794 with instructions written by Hamilton at Washington's behest. Unbeknownst to all sides, Federalist defense policies were about to strengthen Jay's hand. In 1791 Native Americans had inflicted a crushing defeat on U.S. general Arthur St. Clair's ragtag, paid-by-the-day militia: of 52 U.S. officers, 39 were killed and 7 were wounded; of 920 enlisted men, only 24 survived; and scores of women and children were massacred. The debacle finally convinced Congress to grant the long-standing request by Washington and Hamilton for a standing army, a proposal that had been stymied by the Republicans' wariness of strong executive military power.

Secretary of War Henry Knox subsequently organized a professional army of 5,120 men. Based on the Roman legions of Julius Caesar, it was broken into four autonomous military units combining infantry, artillery, and cavalry. In November 1794 the new army had achieved a decisive military victory at the Battle of Falling Timbers (near modern-day Toledo, Ohio), thereby shattering the Native American forces around the Great Lakes area.

Because of the U.S. army's improved performance, and eager to avoid a ground war, the British made a major concession: they would agree to the American demand to remove ten British forts from U.S. territory around the Great Lakes. Britain had promised to do this as part of the Treaty of Paris at the end of the Revolutionary War but had subsequently refused to do so until it was compensated for pre–Revolutionary War debt and the lost financial assets of American loyalists, as promised in the peace treaty.

Britain made several other concessions. London would pay reparations for many of the U.S. commercial ships seized by the Royal Navy while trading with France and would issue a new order in council making it easier for American owners to appeal confiscated vessels in British courts. Britain also agreed to submit prewar debts for arbitration rather than demand a fixed sum. Britain made additional modest trade concessions regarding tariffs and U.S. access to trade with India and the British West Indies. But Jay did not push for an end to impressment, knowing that London would not compromise on something that was necessary for the expansion of the British navy.

Unbeknownst to the Americans, the Jay Treaty had another major benefit. It convinced Spain that a U.S.-British alliance had been established—which was not true—and that Madrid would have to make major territorial compromises to the Americans to forestall a U.S.-British attack against Spanish Florida (consisting of today's Florida and southern Alabama and Louisiana, south of 31 degrees). In negotiations with the U.S. envoy to Spain, Thomas Pinckney, Madrid therefore agreed that U.S. farmers could export their goods through Spanish territory on the Mississippi River unhindered and deposit them in New Orleans free of charge before re-exporting them on sailing ships, a vital American economic interest. Spain also renounced its territorial claims north of the Florida territory all the way to the Ohio River.

Despite British concessions, the treaty caused an uproar back home because it did not end impressment and trade restrictions with Europe. Critics pointed out that the treaty also did not achieve full access to the West Indies–Europe trade, something the colonies had enjoyed before independence. A guileful Washington therefore submitted the treaty to the Federalist-dominated Senate in secret to avoid controversy in the spring of 1795. However, a Republican senator sold his copy to the French ambassador, who gave it to a Republican newspaper for publication.

Riots immediately broke out. A rock struck Hamilton on the head as he defended the treaty in New York City; a hostile mob surrounded Washington's house in Philadelphia. Jay quipped that he was so unpopular that the burning of his effigy illuminated the entire East Coast at night.

Urged on by Jefferson in Monticello, Madison insisted that the Republican-dominated House would have to vote on the treaty since the House would have to provide funding for its implementation. Few thought it would pass. However, with the encouragement of Washington, Hamilton — now back in New York as a lawyer — launched his third famous series of newspaper advocacy articles, "The Defense," under the pen name of Camillus, the fourth-century BC Roman general who saved Rome from Gallic tribes after having withdrawn from public life in the face of an uncomprehending citizenry.

Hamilton's main theme was the need for realism and prudence: "It is not for young and weak nations to attempt to enforce novelties.... [We should] exert all our prudence and address to keep out of war as long as it should be possible to defer, to a state of manhood, a struggle to which infancy is ill adapted.... True honor is a rational thing. It is distinguishable from Quixotism as true courage from the spirit of bravo.... Honor cannot be wounded by consulting moderation."[18] In other words, the United States should put up with the impressment of sailors on U.S. commercial ships: as distasteful as it was, it was not worth endangering the existence of the fragile union by going to war.

As Hamilton's thirty-eight Camillus articles analyzing the treaty's concrete advantages wore away at the Republican opposition, Jefferson lamented to Madison from Monticello, "Hamilton is really a colossus to the anti-republican party. Without numbers he is a host within himself."[19] Washington's low-key but sustained support for the treaty was also decisive. The beginning of the withdrawal of British forts from U.S. territory also had a positive impact on public opinion, particularly in the states near the Great Lakes.

As a result, the treaty passed narrowly in April 1796. True to the Republicans' suspicion of an emerging modern economy, Madison blamed urban interests: "Aristocracy, Anglicism, and mercantilism" led by "the Banks, the British Merchants, and the insurance Companies." Jefferson inveighed privately against Washington, "the one man who outweighs them all in influence over the people," quoting to Madison a line from Washington's own favorite play, *Cato*, "A curse on his virtues, they've undone his country."[20]

Washington never forgave either man for opposing the Jay Treaty. He exchanged some frosty letters with Jefferson after it was approved, writing, "It would not be frank, candid or friendly to conceal that your conduct has been represented [to me] as derogatory." Washington criticized the Republicans for accusing him of being a "Nero" or a "common pickpocket." Jefferson continued to write to Washington for another year about the agricultural economy of Virginia, avoiding all political issues. Washington responded on the same subject until a letter of Jefferson's comparing Washington to a blind Samson was printed, whereupon their correspondence ended.[21]

In September 1796 Washington defended the Jay Treaty in his Farewell Address, which was largely drafted by Hamilton, criticizing implicitly the Republicans for siding with republican France in the belief that the end of monarchy would inaugurate a new era of virtue in international relations. The Farewell Address was also a veiled appeal to discard the outdated 1778 alliance with France and to vote for the Federalist John Adams over Jefferson in 1796: "It is our true policy to steer clear of permanent alliances."

Interestingly, Washington's ego, which had threatened the revolutionary cause after the defeat on the New York battlefield in 1776, surfaced again during the drafting of the Farewell Address. In the initial draft, he wrote, "I did not seek the office with which you have honored me . . . [and now possess] the grey hairs of a man who has [spent] All of the prime of his life—in serving his country; [may he] be suffered to pass quietly to the grave—and that his errors, however, numerous, if they are not criminal, may be consigned to the Tomb of oblivion." Hamilton removed these personal references and moved the entire passage to the end of the speech to make it more of a dignified farewell than a defensive fit of pique. Washington thanked Hamilton for rendering him "with less egotism."[22]

Washington's Farewell Address embodied the political realism of the eighteenth century—cool and cerebral. Washington's favorite noun, *interest*, was mentioned five times; phrases relating to international commerce three times; and the word *justice*, pertaining to international affairs, only once.

The only negative result of the Jay Treaty was that it goaded France into more aggressive policies in the erroneous belief that the United States had entered into an alliance with Britain. Thus, French vessels stepped up their attacks on American merchant ships, particularly in the Caribbean, during the John Adams administration. Ironically, U.S. and British cooperation on convoys helped to foil the French attacks, again demonstrating the need for the flexibility advocated by the Farewell Address. In any case, France's actions during the Adams period showed that Jefferson's hopes for a brotherhood of republics had been naïve; Hamilton's views that nations usually act, or at least should act, out of hardheaded self-interest, not ideology, had been vindicated.

This is not to say that the diplomacy practiced by Washington and Hamilton was flawless. They probably overreacted to France's increased naval harassment during the Adams administration by calling for an expansion of the army to defend against an unlikely French land attack (a threat that did become more real, however, under Napoleon), thereby needlessly stoking Republican fears of the central government. Moreover, Hamilton, while out of power during the Adams administration, generally pushed for policies that were excessively confrontational toward France. While he had warned Washington about letting his ego get in the way of his farewell speech, his own self-regard and personal dislike of Adams may have caused him to challenge Adams's caution toward France. In any case, Adams, whom Washington and Hamilton had supported against Jefferson, struck the right balance by pushing back cautiously against French naval harassment without launching a full-fledged war. The United States could not challenge Britain or France head-on at this point, let alone both of them.

Presidents Jefferson and Madison: The Uncertainties of Power

Jefferson and Madison were more aggressive than Washington and Hamilton in trying to counter British impressment and trade policies, but they seriously misread the balance of military and economic capabilities and of political will between the United States and Britain. Jefferson committed the cardinal error of failing to link military means with his ambitious political goals.

In 1801, his first year in office, Jefferson cut the U.S. military's five-million-dollar budget on the grounds that a strong navy, which received 40 percent of the budget, could drag the United States into a war at sea and that the taxes for defense would strengthen the central government, the perennial fear of Virginia and the southern states. Given these reductions, four individuals refused Jefferson's offer to be secretary of the navy; he finally settled upon a nonentity, Robert Smith, who owed his job to the fact that he was the brother of a powerful senator. Jefferson ordered Smith to fire two-thirds of enlisted navy personnel and mothball most U.S. oceangoing frigates. In their place, Jefferson funded the construction of flimsy gunboats manned by citizen volunteers to protect U.S. harbors. The gunboats were prone to capsize outside of the ports, and their guns were of little use.

The defense cuts were made just as British maritime policies were getting tougher in response to the rise of a hegemonic France. By 1805 Napoleon ruled most of Western Europe after his decisive victories over the Austrian Empire and the Austrian-Russian coalition at Ulm and Austerlitz respectively. Only the British fleet, which had defeated a French-Spanish fleet at Trafalgar the same year, and perhaps Russia, stood between Napoleon and an empire that rivaled that of Rome.

In response to Napoleon's military triumphs on land, London sought to tighten its naval blockade of French-dominated Europe, including increased restrictions on U.S. trade with Europe. British decrees mandated that U.S. commercial vessels could only trade with Europe if American goods passed through British ports and paid duties; as many as two out of nine U.S. merchant ships heading toward Europe were forced to stop temporarily in British ports. Under the so-called Rule of 1756, British lawyers argued that in wartime neutrals such as the United States had the right to continue their peacetime trade patterns but could not profit from new trade opportunities created by the war. Napoleon issued similar decrees directed at U.S. ships trading with Britain, but his smaller navy was less of a hindrance to U.S. commerce.

Despite the new restrictions, U.S. merchant ships still made enormous profits from their trade with Europe in large part because they had replaced French, Spanish, and Dutch merchant vessels, which were driven from the seas by the British. Moreover, U.S. ship captains could often evade British restrictions through smuggling and false papers. Finally, both Britain and France sold licenses exempting U.S. vessels from the new trade regulations. In fact, the British had a certain interest in allowing Napoleon to buy U.S. agricultural products because it diverted hard currency from more lethal purposes. In short, U.S. commerce continued to prosper: the volume of trade would not reach the heights of the Napoleonic wars again until a century later.[23]

Unlike the Federalists, Jefferson believed he had an effective option with economic sanctions against Britain. Yet the policy was built on wishful thinking that overrated the importance of America's modest trade with Europe in items that were not essential to the war effort such as cotton, sugar, and tobacco. U.S. timber exports were important for shipbuilding, and Jefferson thought that Napoleon's conquest of the Baltic states, where Britain got most of its supplies, would leave Britain vulnerable. However, this ignored Canada, where timber exports to Britain boomed.

Despite the modest prospects for success, Congress, with Jefferson's support, passed the weak Non-Importation Act in 1806 that banned the importation of some British goods. Jefferson promptly suspended its implementation to give diplomacy a chance. What was meant as a sign of resolve must have come across to London as ambivalence and uncertainty.

Jefferson then directed the Republican James Monroe, the U.S. minister to Britain, and William Pinkney, the former Federalist politician, to negotiate an end to British trade levies and impressment. During the negotiations, the British did make several gestures of conciliation. They offered to renew the trade concessions made in the Jay Treaty and to exercise greater caution when impressing seamen. In 1806 Jefferson turned down the proposed Monroe-Pinkney Treaty, which the Federalists probably would have accepted as they had the Jay Treaty, because it did not end all impressment and ease all trade restrictions. Jefferson had made the perfect enemy of the good, thereby missing a major opportunity to reduce tensions.

The *Chesapeake-Leopard* affair reflected Jefferson's clumsy uncertainties in evaluating the military balance of power between the United States and Britain. In June 1807 the British naval ship H.M.S. *Leopard* fired several naval shells, a rare resort to outright force against a U.S. vessel, into the U.S.S. *Chesapeake*, which had around one hundred British subjects in its crew, in international waters off Norfolk, Virginia. The British boarding party then removed four deserters from British ships, one of whom was later hanged. British foreign secretary George Canning subsequently told Monroe in London that the shelling and boarding had been unauthorized and that the three remaining men would be released and an indemnity would be paid. But a prideful and naïve Jefferson turned down the offer, hoping that he could use the adverse political reaction in the United States to the attack to threaten a war he did not intend in order to obtain an end to impressment, something that Canning refused to even discuss. The political storm in the United States soon subsided as trade interests reasserted themselves; the three remaining seamen remained under British control.

With the failure of the halfhearted Non-Importation Act, Jefferson flailed around for another option, this time settling on an embargo of U.S. exports to Britain in December 1807. Jefferson assured political leaders that the embargo would keep American sailors out of harm's way and would force Britain to give way to American demands within a year.

Britain shrugged off the embargo as a nuisance; London could live without U.S. trade, and fewer U.S. merchant ships crossing the Atlantic meant more work for the British merchant marine. Evasion was widespread: all of a sudden, American merchant ships left New York harbor with full cargoes for "the Azores," not exactly a huge trading hub. In fact, the most serious damage caused by the embargo was not against England but against the East Coast economies. As a result, Federalists doubled their representation in the 1808 congressional elections.[24]

Ironically, the Democratic-Republicans, who had thought that the end of the French monarchy in 1792 would help usher in a more peaceful world, were now drifting toward the very war that their political realist rivals, the Federalists, had avoided. Madison, like Jefferson, floundered around with ineffective on-again, off-again economic sanctions during the first years of his administration. When this failed to change British policy, President Madison decided to invade Canada. The goal was not to annex it, which would have upset the balance between the northern and southern states, but to inflict enough pain to force Britain to desist from its maritime policies. Madison foresaw an easy victory and retired to his estate for his annual summer vacation the day after declaring war in June 1812; Jefferson felt the same and looked forward to negotiating an end to British maritime interference.

Unlike Washington and Hamilton in the 1780s and 1790s, Madison and Jefferson displayed poor strategic judgment in their misreading of the military, political, and economic realities. First, the military situation did not favor the United States. Madison had a weak army and navy in part because he and Jefferson had cut the defense budget since 1800. The United States had sixteen naval vessels to Britain's six hundred and fewer than seven thousand army regulars to Britain's half a million. Moreover, Madison and Jefferson seemed to have forgotten the lessons from the American Revolutionary War, when the United States had failed in its attempt to annex Canada. French Canadians would presumably remain largely neutral again, and most Anglo-Canadians remained loyal to Britain (in part because they saw London as protecting them from French Canadians). If anything, the ranks of pro-British Canadians had grown with the influx of American loyalists who had left the United States after independence.

Second, U.S. public opinion was ambivalent about hostilities. A declaration of war passed narrowly in Congress with the New England trading states strongly opposed. Yet the main routes for attacking the most populated areas of Canada, particularly Montreal, required going through New England. In fact, New England had been cutting its own deals with Britain to avoid U.S. trade restrictions under Jefferson and Madison; to imagine it would supply military personnel was even more misguided.

Third, the British would have been willing to make meaningful compromises if Jefferson and Madison had met them halfway. To avoid war with the United States, Britain repealed the orders in council in 1812 that had restricted U.S. trade with Europe and led to impressments. But the news arrived after Congress had narrowly declared war on Britain with Madison's urging.

Finally, Madison and Jefferson failed to understand the implications of Napoleon's imminent invasion of Russia, which the U.S. ambassador to Russia, John Quincy Adams, was aware of in the summer of 1812. If Napoleon's invasion ended in his defeat, Britain could send more military forces to North America—which is what happened. Conversely, if Napoleon emerged victorious, then the United States would have to consider joining Britain to prevent Napoleon from turning again toward conquering North America. Either way, this was *not* the time to declare war on Britain.

Madison's invasion of Canada went poorly. Smaller but more effective British and Canadian forces repulsed several ineffectual American forays into Canada during the first two years of the war. The well-trained British professionals fought better than the American militia units, and Canadian militia frequently outperformed the Americans because they were defending their own territory. Treasury Secretary Albert Gallatin wrote to Jefferson that the "misfortune" of "our military land operations exceeded all anticipations." Senator Henry Clay wrote to a friend, "Mr. Madison is wholly unfit for the storms of War. . . . Nature has cast him in too benevolent a mold."[25]

Despite isolated naval victories on Lake Erie and in the Atlantic by the U.S.S. *Constitution*, the war at sea went even more badly for the Americans. In 1813 the Royal Navy blockaded Charleston, Savannah, and New York City, thereby devastating those economies. The British blockade also forced merchants to abandon the cheap and fast coastal maritime trade in favor of the more expensive and slower inland roads. As Napoleon's position continued to decline, the British were able to shift more forces to North America to conduct punishing coastal attacks with naval and ground forces, culminating in the burning of Washington in 1814.

Most seriously, the war threatened the very unity of the newly formed United States. New England merchants traded freely with Britain; New England banks probably loaned more money to the British than to their own compatriots during the war. During the first two years of the war, the British government, which needed American foodstuffs for its army in Spain, did not blockade New England. However, in May 1814, following the abdication of Napoleon, New England was also blockaded. As a result, Federalist officials from New England sought more autonomy for their states on a permanent basis at the Hartford Convention of December 1814 to January 1815. They did not call for outright secession, but they might have done so if the war had continued. With the final fall of Napoleon in the summer of 1815, however, the war came to a rapid end, and with it British trade restrictions and impressment. The war had not been a disaster, but it could have been. Madison had gambled with the nation's future and was lucky not to have lost.

The trajectory of early American diplomacy illustrates many of the key principles of effective statecraft. Washington and Hamilton approached international relations prudently. During the American Revolution, Washington did not get carried away by the alliance with France and turned aside Lafayette's proposal that the French be encouraged to expel the British from Canada. Moreover, during the early years of the French Revolution, Washington and Hamilton had the wisdom to avoid exposing the young American republic to a full-scale conflict with Britain or France because both countries were more powerful militarily and because a war would be too controversial domestically, given the extensive commercial ties with England. Conversely, the potential policy gains of open warfare—defeating the Native Americans in the greater Ohio area who sometimes allied with the British—were modest insofar as the increasing numbers of European settlers would soon overwhelm the Native population.

In fact, the United States had an interest in securing a British and anti-Napoleon coalition victory as quickly as possible. While Britain engaged in more harassment of U.S. ships because it had a stronger navy, even Jefferson realized a united Europe under French leadership represented the greater danger.

Washington and Hamilton were also more judicious than Jefferson and Madison in their matching of policy means to policy ends. They stressed in their letters to each other that the United States had great potential but was still in its early stages of military, political, and economic development. Better therefore to maintain a low profile for several more decades and continue to build national power than to enter a premature full-scale commercial or military conflict. While opposed to war, they favored funding a professional army and oceangoing frigates that could defend the East Coast against Britain and France if necessary.

In contrast, Jefferson and Madison advocated a more muscular foreign policy while declining the military means to implement it; they opposed a professional army and turned against the construction of oceangoing frigates during the 1790s, the very decade when British and French naval harassment began. Their foreign and defense policies contradicted each other.

Jefferson and Madison also indulged in wishful thinking about a range of issues, notably the ability of the United States to use trade and a military invasion of Canada to force the British to desist and the peaceful intensions of the French republic. Intellectual rigor was not their strong point.

Hamilton understood intellectual complexity as well as any political leader in American history. During the 1780s, as noted, he laid out the conceptual case for why republican governments would not necessarily be pacific powers. He felt that three basic factors explained wars irrespective of the forms of government involved, as set forth in his *Federalist* no. 6 (1788): First, nations and peoples are prone to love power either for offensive reasons, the tendency toward domination, or for defensive reasons, the need for safety. Second, commercial rivalries can be a cause of war and not just a web of peaceful interdependence. Third, individual leaders can seek out war for their own political benefit. Because, as he noted, human nature can be "ambitious, vindictive, and rapacious," the American states needed a political union to reduce the likelihood of war among themselves as well as to protect themselves from outside threats. At bottom, Washington and Hamilton did not engage in excessive optimism or pessimism, but they did consider worst-case scenarios.

Hamilton also applied his keen mind to his apprehension about the fate of the French Revolution even during its initial optimistic early days. He cited four specific reasons for his wariness: the resistance of the French nobility to any loss of power, the "vehemence" of the French people, the "reveries of your philosophical politicians," and the inevitable disputes that would revolve around drawing up a new constitution.[26]

Yet again, he displayed his superb analytical skills to promote the strict neutrality policy of 1793 instead of siding with France. As mentioned, he argued that the 1778 alliance with France obligated U.S. assistance only if France were attacked, whereas Paris was now the aggressor. U.S. assistance to France would also be ineffective given America's modest armed forces and would expose it to attack from Britain and its allies. Moreover, as noted, Hamilton's thirty-eight Camillus articles in 1795 analyzing the Jay Treaty's many advantages helped to wear down the Republican opposition. Hamilton's mind was relentless in its ability to disaggregate complicated issues.

In war, Washington demonstrated the ability to learn and adapt after his initial battlefield defeats. Both he and Hamilton displayed boldness and raw physical courage in battle. Washington would encourage his men while on horseback on the frontlines; Hamilton chafed at being a staff aide working in safety and finally convinced Washington to allow him to lead a charge at Yorktown. In contrast, Jefferson and Madison did not convey the image of forceful authority that Washington and Hamilton did. Indeed, the Virginia state legislature called for an investigation of Jefferson's conduct as governor during the Revolutionary War because he had left the state vulnerable to British depredations when he fled Richmond. While the exact truth remains unclear, Jefferson and, to a lesser degree, Madison seem to have been conflict-avoidant in their personal relations.[27]

The prudent statecraft of Washington and Hamilton reflected the intellectual views of the late seventeenth century and eighteenth century, when political realist thinking began to flower as the modern European state system took root. Hamilton read the memoirs of Prussia's King Frederick the Great, who contributed to the political realist tradition in his writings about the national interest of European states; Washington kept a bust of Frederick on his mantelpiece. There was little place for ideology and emotion in this world where the margin of error was narrow, particularly for Prussia, then the weakest of Europe's major powers.

However, an intellectual countercurrent began to develop in eighteenth-century Europe that had an impact on the thinking of the party of Jefferson and Madison. In France in particular, the non-noble classes resented the fact that while they had access to commerce and the professions, they were still excluded from foreign policy and military affairs, the aristocracy's last redoubt. Hence, the non-noble classes saw the eighteenth-century wars as unnecessary games designed to occupy a degenerate aristocracy. If middle-class republics gained power, they would devote themselves to international trade that would weave a network of interdependency and reduce the likelihood of war. Thomas Paine, in his *Rights of Man* (1791–1792), and Immanuel Kant, in his *Perpetual Peace* (1795), would make these optimistic arguments with great eloquence.[28]

Jefferson shared these optimistic views. He wrote to Madison while still in Paris that the West had entered into a new, more civilized era where morality could play a greater role in foreign policy-making. To deny gratitude toward France for its assistance to the United States during the American Revolutionary War was "to revive a principle which has been buried for centuries with its kindred principles of the lawfulness of assassination, poison, perjury, etc. All of these were legitimate principles in the dark ages which intervened between ancient and modern civilization, but exploded and held in just horror in the 18th century."[29]

However, Washington and Hamilton did not idealize the new republican government in France—or their own. In contrast with Jefferson, when war broke out between France and Britain, they decided on a policy of strict neutrality regardless of the 1778 Franco-American alliance. American interests took precedence over nebulous ideals of solidarity among republics. And, in fact, the French Revolution ushered in a new dark age of nationalistic wars of entire peoples and mass armies culminating in the twentieth-century world wars. In any case, Washington and Hamilton understood the complexities of their times, particularly the challenges by Britain and France, and their prudent policy-making earned them the admiration of their greatest successor, Abraham Lincoln.[30]

CHAPTER 3

Abraham Lincoln

The Diplomacy of Prudence

Abraham Lincoln is best known for his success in the Union war effort and for ending slavery. Yet his diplomacy toward Britain and France was also essential for the Northern victory. Lincoln could not have won the war through diplomacy, but he could have lost it if he had blundered into hostilities with Britain and France, as Jefferson and Madison had done half a century earlier.

Lincoln and Secretary of State William Seward faced diplomatic challenges from the start of the war because Britain and France both supported the South. For Britain, a Southern victory would weaken the growing American colossus, which represented a threat to its interests in the western hemisphere, particularly in Canada. London also sought an end to the Northern naval blockade of the Southern states, whose cotton exports fed a vast network of textile mills in the greater Manchester area. Moreover, British leaders, while unsympathetic to slavery in principle, feared that the longer the war dragged on, the greater the likelihood of further disruption to the cotton trade by revolts of enslaved workers.

In addition to concrete interests, most Britons, remembering perhaps their own failure against the American colonies, genuinely believed that the North was engaged in an unwinnable war against a large population in control of a huge territory. The war, therefore, should end as soon as possible for humanitarian purposes. Moreover, much of the British elite identified with the "aristocratic" South and

41

disliked the more unruly "democratic" North, which it associated with its own property-less citizens, who were agitating for the right to vote. Finally, British foreign policy generally supported the concept of self-determination in international affairs and felt this applied to the South.

At the same time, Britain held off extending formal diplomatic recognition to the Confederacy and intervening militarily on its behalf for several reasons. London was afraid that the North could retaliate against Canada, and Britons valued their extensive trade in grains, saltpeter, and arms with the Northern states as well as their investments there. British leaders also had to take into consideration the antislavery sympathies in their own country. Ironically, it was the English working classes, whose livelihoods depended on Southern cotton, who were most opposed to the Southern cause. They identified with oppressed peoples in general. And, as Hamilton had pointed out in his writings, emotions play an important role in politics as well as concrete interests.

France also had its reasons to favor the Confederate states. France depended on Southern cotton for its textile industry, although less so than Britain. More important, Napoleon III had ambitions to establish a client state in Mexico to serve as a hub for an informal French empire in Latin America. Economic interests and a desire to compete with his more famous uncle drove his policy. Hoping to replicate the recent British-French partnership in the Crimean War, Napoleon, however, was reluctant to intervene militarily against the powerful Union states without British support.

How did the inexperienced President Lincoln deal with British and French designs? His contemporaries tended to disparage his importance and abilities in diplomacy. Lincoln's envoy to Britain, Charles Francis Adams, the son of John Quincy Adams, thought the president was a hayseed who deferred to his secretary of state on international affairs. Adams's own son recounted the only meeting that his father had with Lincoln and Seward thus: "Presently a door opened and a tall, large-featured, shabbily dressed man of uncouth appearance slouched into the room. . . . Lincoln remarked that it was to 'Governor Seward' rather than to himself that Mr. Adams should express any sense of obligation. Then, stretching out his legs before him, he said with an air of relief . . . 'Well Governor, I've this morning decided that Chicago post office appointment.'" This view of Lincoln as a disengaged amateur was widely shared among much of the diplomatic corps, including the British ambassador Lord Richard Lyons and the British press.[1]

The true picture was more complicated. Lincoln knew, at a minimum, that British and French recognition of the Confederacy would boost the South's morale and demoralize the North. Actual military intervention, probably in the form of British and French ships trying to break up the naval blockade to gain access to cotton, could have a major impact on the Southern economy, including its ability to import European arms. The North therefore could not afford conflict with either country. This would be Lincoln's guiding diplomatic principle, as he stressed in numerous conversations.

Lincoln came to understand the nuances of the period's diplomacy as well as its broad contours. He read the reporting from U.S. diplomats in London and Paris, who wrote extensively about the impact of the slavery issue and the cotton trade on the British and French governments and public opinion. He also developed a sophisticated understanding of British interests and the parliamentary system, including which potential coalitions would best serve U.S. interests. In 1864 an English barrister, George Borrett, recorded that the president spoke to him knowledgeably about the British legal system, including arcana about the rights of neutrals and belligerents during wartime.[2]

Lincoln spent more time with Seward than he did with any of his other cabinet officials in part because these officials had consuming administrative and policy duties. Seward, for his part, frequently noted in his outgoing cables to U.S. envoys abroad that the president had decided on a particular foreign policy.[3]

Lincoln sometimes overruled Seward, though he respected the former New York state governor, who had the benefit of having traveled to Europe and having met with British prime minister Henry John Temple, Lord Palmerston, in 1859. In February 1861 Seward, who could be aggressive, spoke openly at Washington dinner parties about how a foreign war could reunite the North and South after the six southernmost states seceded on February 4. On April 1 Seward wrote a memo, "Thoughts for the President's Consideration," proposing that the United States demand "explanations" from Spain, presumably about its interest in re-annexing Santo Domingo, and from France, presumably about its moves toward the occupation of Haiti, as a pretext for declaring war. Lincoln turned the proposal aside and told Republican politician Carl Schurz in late spring that he needed to devote more time to foreign affairs.[4]

Lincoln demonstrated an attitude more prudent than Seward's in a second incident. On May 13, 1861, Britain declared neutrality between the two American "belligerent" parties. The move did not constitute diplomatic recognition, but it did allow Confederate ships to obtain coal, arms, supplies, and repairs and to contract loans in Britain. Other European powers followed the British lead. Seward also learned that British foreign minister John Russell had met with three Confederate envoys in late April. The envoys asked for British diplomatic recognition, and Russell told them that the cabinet would discuss the issue; British newspapers reported that diplomatic recognition was in the air.

Seward drafted the May 21 dispatch, a cable stating that diplomatic recognition could mean war between the United States and Britain. Lincoln toned down the draft and instructed Adams to use it for guidance in his meeting with Russell rather than present the still strongly worded message directly to the British foreign minister. Russell told Adams that he had seen the envoys twice, which was true, but did not plan to see them again; he would see another Confederate envoy in 1862.

In July Lincoln again demonstrated his cautious attitude toward Britain. He ignored a congressional bill empowering him to close Southern ports that were not yet subject to the blockade, which was at that point limited by the number of naval vessels. While Britain had promised to respect the blockade, it insisted that it had the right under international law to trade with unblockaded ports and would not allow Northern naval ships to detain or search British vessels on the high seas that had traded with such ports. Lincoln told U.S. senator Orville Browning that he did not want a war with Britain over the issue.[5]

Most important, Lincoln, as well as Seward, exercised prudence during what became known as the *Trent* affair, the most dangerous foreign confrontation of the Civil War. The incident involved a series of unpredictable occurrences that almost led to war in November and December 1861, illustrating the role of chance in history. Ironically, the confrontation began in part because the first Confederate envoy,

William Yancey, had gotten nowhere with the British government since his initial meetings with Foreign Minister Russell in the spring of 1861 and wanted to resign. President Jefferson Davis appointed two former U.S. senators to be new envoys, James Mason to Britain and John Slidell to France. In October 1861 Mason and Slidell escaped the Union blockade of Charleston harbor and headed to Cuba to board the next British mail packet, the *Trent*. By chance, a Union naval captain, Charles Wilkes, was temporarily in Cuba with his ship the *San Jacinto* when he learned about their plans from the newspapers. Wilkes had a reputation for being a stubborn and impulsive braggart. He may have also held a grudge against Slidell, with whom he had quarreled over a girl when they were schoolboys in New York.

Without authorization from Washington, Wilkes fired warning shots at the *Trent* on November 8 after it departed from Havana and ordered his executive officer, Lieutenant D. M. Fairfax, to lead a boarding party. Fairfax removed Mason and Slidell but acquiesced when the British ship captain said his men would resist a search of the ship for contraband, including any Confederate diplomatic dispatches. With Mason and Slidell under his control, Wilkes became an overnight hero to the Northern public as news of his exploit spread quickly by telegraph. Secretary of the Navy Gideon Welles sent him a letter of congratulations, Congress passed a resolution praising him, and legal experts opined that the move was lawful. The public finally had a success after seven months of Union defeats.

In fact, under international law Wilkes should have taken the entire ship, including the envoys, to the nearest prize court in the United States to consider the legal status of the ship, its passengers, and contents. (Prize courts were federal courts that ruled on the legality of seizures of neutral ships engaged in trade with the Southern states.) However, in this particular case, Fairfax convinced Wilkes to let the *Trent* continue to Britain because the *San Jacinto* was needed for an upcoming attack on Port Royal, South Carolina, and also perhaps to avoid an international incident. The subsequent British legal protest was based in part on Wilkes's unilateral decision to arrest only the two envoys rather than escort the entire ship to a prize court for adjudication.

The British cabinet, assuming erroneously that Wilkes was acting under instructions from the U.S. government, demanded the release of Mason and Slidell and a formal apology. British hostility was exacerbated when envoy Lord Lyons stressed in his reporting that Seward was looking for a fight and that Lincoln did not count in foreign affairs. To compel Washington to give way, the British cabinet decided to prohibit the export from India of saltpeter, a key component of explosives for the North. More ominously, the cabinet also ordered the military reinforcement of Canada and the western hemisphere. On December 6 three battleships, a frigate, and a corvette were sent to Bermuda from the Mediterranean and Channel fleets; on December 9 the cabinet decided to add ten thousand troops to the five thousand already in Canada. The British war department drew up plans to occupy Maine in order to draw Northern troops away from the main line of presumed attack toward Montreal and Toronto.

While the British cabinet believed the North would have the upper hand in a land war, they were confident that their own forces enjoyed naval superiority. Some government officials believed burning New York and Boston was a viable option; Queen Victoria told her uncle that there would be "utter destruction to the North Americans."[6] Moreover, British public opinion was firmly behind the war option unless the Americans gave way on the *Trent* affair. An American observer in London, Thurlow Weed, wrote, "There is with but few individual exceptions, but one voice here. All are for war, first on account of the Honor of the Flag, and next because they think we want to quarrel with them."[7] Even after learning that Wilkes had acted without authorization, the British assumed that war was possible because Wilkes had become such a hero in the North.

In case of war, the first objective of British admiral Alexander Milne, the commander of North American forces, would be to establish coaling stations in Southern ports and destroy the Northern blockade. How realistic were these plans? The Americans had more naval vessels, but most were jerry-rigged commercial sailing craft. All the British vessels were steamships, and London planned to send its best vessels to the western hemisphere in case of hostilities since there were no other overriding crises in the world.

Lincoln and Seward acted cautiously throughout the entire incident, in contrast to Secretary Welles, who, as usual, dismissed British protests as empty posturing. Seward sent a message to Adams in

London on November 30 stating that Wilkes had acted on his own. On December 2 Lincoln did not mention the wildly popular incident in his written address to Congress while stating that the United States had been pursuing a policy of "prudence" in its relations with foreign powers, thereby signaling to Britain that he was not seeking a fight. On December 4 Lincoln told a visiting British official from Canada that he wanted no quarrel with London.

Washington received news of the British demands on December 15. On December 22 Senator Charles Sumner, head of the Senate Foreign Relations Committee, told Lincoln that Britain had the ability to break the blockade and help establish an independent Confederacy. Lincoln told Sumner in response that there would be no war unless Britain wanted one. Privately, he told his friend James Gilmore, "I lay awake all night, contriving how to get out of the scrape without loss of national dignity." Lincoln also told Attorney General Edward Bates, "I am not getting much sleep out of that exploit of Wilkes. I am not much of a prize lawyer, but it seems to me pretty clear that . . . Wilkes . . . has no right to turn his quarter-deck into a prize court."[8]

On December 25 and 26 the cabinet decided that the United States would have to meet the British demands. On January 1, 1862, Mason and Slidell and their two secretaries were taken on a tugboat from their prison in Boston to Provincetown; London made a point of sending a warship to pick them up from the vessel. Lyons's message about their release was announced in London theaters on January 9 to cheering audiences. With a break in diplomatic relations or war no longer probable, Adams noted dryly in his diary, "I am to remain in this purgatory a while longer."[9] Southern leaders were surprised and bitterly disappointed by the resolution of the impasse; General Robert E. Lee was one of the few Confederates who had foreseen the outcome.[10]

While the *Trent* affair represented the most dangerous single international incident during the war, Lincoln and Steward faced Britain's growing concern about the sharp decline in cotton exports. The South had always thought that a cotton shortage would force Britain to intervene, perhaps even militarily, since a significant portion of its workforce in the Manchester region depended on cotton for textile production. However, during the first year of the war there were only modest disruptions in the cotton supply in Britain. Cotton inventories were already high; British authorities were able to shift some cotton production to India, Egypt, and Turkey; and the Northern blockade was still somewhat porous. By the summer of 1862, however, supplies stood at one-third the normal level as inventories ran down and the blockade became more effective.

Lincoln and Seward were aware of the growing economic pressures in Britain through Adams's reporting and the British press. Partly as a result, Lincoln informed his cabinet on July 22, 1862, that he intended to issue a declaration of emancipation for the enslaved individuals in the Southern states that had seceded, though not in the border states that remained in the Union. Seward supported the proposal but advised its postponement "until you can give it to the country supported by military success. Otherwise, the world might consider it as our last measure of an exhausted government, a cry for help . . . our last shriek. On the retreat." Seward's advice "struck me with very great force," said the president later.[11]

Meanwhile, Lord Palmerston sidelined a parliamentary resolution in support of recognition, though a majority of Parliament's members favored it. He wrote to Foreign Minister Russell, however, on September 14, that he would consider such a step if Lee's upcoming offensive into Maryland succeeded. After the Northern victory at Antietam later that month, Palmerston argued to the cabinet that Britain should still hold back; the cabinet voted to support the prime minister against Russell and Chancellor of the Exchequer William Gladstone. One of Palmerston's biographers, W. Baring Pemberton, captured the prime minister's state of mind:

> An older and more cautious Palmerston now occupied the stage. At forty-seven, he might have played for high stakes, using the threat of an alliance with the South and war with the North to break the blockade, bring hostilities to an end, and, flourishing the sanction of trade concessions, achieve something toward the end of slavery. At seventy-seven, he was very willing to be persuaded by Cobden's argument that it would be cheaper to feed Lancashire's unemployed every day on "turtle, champagne and venison" than to embark on a war with the United States. Tired, aging, uncertain of his majority, Palmerston was in no mind to lead the country to war.[12]

Lincoln was not aware of the specific state of political play in Britain, but he knew enough to tell a delegation of Chicago clergy in mid-September that "to proclaim emancipation would secure the sympathy of Europe . . . which now saw no other reason for the strife than national pride and ambition. No other step would be as potent to prevent foreign intervention."[13] And with the Southern invasion of Maryland stopped at Antietam, Lincoln announced on September 22 that he would issue the Emancipation Proclamation on January 1, 1863. By Christmas diplomatic and press articles had begun to arrive in Washington about the proclamation's favorable impact in Europe. The son of U.S. envoy Charles Adams wrote from London, "The Emancipation Proclamation has done more for us here than all our former victories and all our diplomacy. It is creating an almost convulsive reaction in our favor all over this country." Seward noted that Lincoln was "disposed to take a more cheering view of our foreign relations at this time than he has allowed himself to indulge at any previous period since the civil war commenced."[14]

During 1863, Lincoln and Steward continued to combine prudence, occasional threats, and appeals to idealism to reduce tensions with Britain. Lincoln held off implementing a congressional bill that authorized U.S. private vessels, the privateers, to seize British blockade runners. Moreover, Lincoln ordered Secretary of the Navy Welles to avoid using neutral ports such as Saint Thomas as launch points from which to stop British ships suspected of carrying contraband. Lincoln also overruled Welles, who believed that mail should be seized on British and French ships, not just arms and munitions; Lincoln told Welles that "his object was to 'keep the peace,' for we could not afford to take upon ourselves a war with England and France, which was threatened if we stopped their mails."[15]

Lincoln and Seward did harden their tone, however, when they learned about a new generation of iron-class ships under construction in Liverpool for sale to the Confederacy. Unlike the limited amounts of contraband small arms and munitions that made their way through the blockade on small wooden vessels, these new iron vessels, both the North and the South believed, could severely undermine the blockade. Seward therefore told Adams to inform London that Washington would consider authorizing American privateers for the first time to seize British commercial vessels if the new ships were sold to the South. In September Russell informed Adams that while Britain could not legally prevent the advanced ironclads from being built in Liverpool, as Seward demanded, the British government would purchase them for their own navy, thereby keeping them out of the Civil War.

Lincoln also appealed to British idealists. In April he drafted a resolution that was sent to John Bright, the antislavery political leader, for use in his rallies: "Whereas . . . an attempt has been made to construct a new nation upon the basis of . . . human slavery . . . Resolved, that no such embryo state, should ever be recognized by, or admitted into, the family of Christian and civilized nations." Lincoln's words then were heard across the Atlantic in rallies across Britain.[16]

Lincoln's diplomacy, along with Northern victories in Gettysburg and Vicksburg, laid to rest the specter of British diplomatic and military intervention by the end of 1863. And while French military forces were still in Mexico, Napoleon III, as mentioned previously, never considered direct military intervention without Britain. Hence, Northern diplomacy had isolated the South from its potential allies in Europe.[17]

Lincoln was an effective wartime leader for a number of reasons, including his ability to operate in different spheres of action simultaneously. As the commander in chief he was aggressive and demanding. He pushed military commanders hard because he knew that if they did not destroy Lee's army, the South would probably eventually outlast the North, where public opinion was susceptible to some form of compromise peace, as advocated by Lincoln's rival in the 1864 election, former General George McClellan. He removed five Northern commanders for not being aggressive enough before settling on Ulysses Grant, known as the butcher because of his implacable nature. General Grant was known, in fact, to avoid visiting wounded soldiers during the Civil War because he feared it would undermine his determination to pursue the war aggressively. With the fate of the war in the balance in the summer of 1864, Lincoln urged Grant to "hold on with a bulldog grip, and chew and choke as much as possible."[18]

At the same time, Lincoln was cautious in his diplomacy. He grasped that he could not afford to provoke Britain, and with it France, into recognizing the South's independence because the next step could be an attempt to break the blockade. He restrained Seward on several occasions and ignored congressional authorizations and Secretary Welles's dismissal of British warnings about their maritime rights, including during the all-important *Trent* affair.

The policies of political leaders flow from their personalities: aggressive personalities may be prone to excessive force, while cautious individuals may tend to be too restrained. What Lincoln succeeded in doing was operating simultaneously in two different modes: forceful as commander in chief, but prudent as diplomat. Sometimes he used the iron fist and sometimes the velvet glove in a period when there was no margin for error and iron and velvet were both needed.

CHAPTER 4

Theodore Roosevelt

From Nationalist to Realist

Theodore Roosevelt's foreign policy lends itself easily either to hagiography or hostile caricature. American advocates of the robust use of military force often cite Roosevelt as a model statesman who wielded military power unapologetically to establish America as a world power during and after the Spanish-American War. His appealing swagger, in their view, was epitomized by what came to be known as the Perdicaris incident in 1904. Ion Perdicaris, an American citizen living in Tangiers, was taken hostage by a Moroccan warlord, Ahmad Raisuli. Raisuli threatened to kill Perdicaris to extort money and political concessions from the Sultan of Morocco. The Roosevelt administration issued a demand to the Moroccan authorities, "We want Perdicaris alive or Raisuli dead," and sent naval ships to Tangiers to back up the statement.[1] Critics of an assertive U.S. foreign policy, however, often criticize Roosevelt for making the Philippines a protectorate and for carving Panama out of Colombia. For them, Roosevelt never met a war he did not like.

While there is some truth in both of these viewpoints, they apply mainly to the young Roosevelt. Like Washington on the battlefield, Roosevelt moved away from his early impetuousness and toward a prudent diplomacy captured by his well-known injunction, "Speak softly and carry a big stick."[2]

Certainly, the young Roosevelt exuded aggressiveness. Sickly and asthmatic as a boy, he took up boxing as a teenager in response to being bullied. By his twenties he had developed a reputation as a walking battering ram who once leaped off a horse into a pack of hounds and knifed a cougar to death. A former college friend remembered Roosevelt as a student at Harvard: "He would like above all things to go to war with someone. He has just walked out of the hotel with a rifle over his shoulder. . . . He . . . wants to be killing something all the time."[3]

As an undergraduate at Harvard, Roosevelt chose to do his senior thesis on the naval war of 1812 between the United States and Britain. When told that he could not graduate with honors if he wrote about military history, he went ahead and wrote it anyway. In his thesis he demonstrated an incisive understanding of the complexity of naval warfare, including putting himself in the shoes of an adversary, the British navy. The thesis was so highly regarded that it was published as a book, *The Naval War of 1812*. The book sold well, and the U.S. Navy made it required reading.

The book's success ushered Roosevelt into a circle of military intellectuals such as Alfred Thayer Mahan, a historian and strong supporter of naval power. Roosevelt easily took to the prevailing worldview of those intellectuals whose Victorian political ideology of "Anglo-Saxonism" posited that European peoples, and particularly those in northern Europe and North America, had a right and duty to expand throughout the world to spread their superior institutions and values.

To this end, Roosevelt and his close friends, such as Senator Henry Cabot Lodge of Massachusetts, believed that the United States should pursue an aggressive expansionist foreign policy. In 1889 several U.S. and German naval ships confronted each other for six months in the Samoan harbor during the Samoan Civil War. Roosevelt wrote to his British friend Cecil Spring Rice, "Frankly I don't know that I should be sorry to see a bit of a spar with Germany. The burning of New York and a few other sea coast cities would be a good object lesson in the need of an adequate system of coast defenses and I think it would have a good effect on our large German population to force them to an ostentatiously patriotic display of anger against Germany."[4]

Similarly, as a New York State politician Roosevelt cheered on the Cleveland administration when it sided against the United Kingdom in 1895 in a border dispute between British Guiana and Venezuela. Roosevelt mused in a letter to his son-in-law, "I earnestly hope our government do'n't [sic] back down. If there is a muss I shall try to have a hand in it myself! They'll have to employ a lot of men just as green as I am even for the conquest of Canada."[5] One of his friends in New York State politics deplored his "very juvenile fashion" about the incident.[6]

Roosevelt's views on geopolitics began to have a concrete impact after Senator Lodge lobbied successfully for Roosevelt's appointment as assistant secretary of the navy following William McKinley's victory in 1896. McKinley admired Roosevelt's dynamism but considered him too pugnacious; Secretary of the Navy John D. Long regarded his deputy as a parent might consider a precocious but wild teenager. In his diary, Long appraised Roosevelt as a man "so enthusiastic and loyal that he is in certain respects invaluable; yet I lack confidence in his good judgment and discretion. [Roosevelt] goes off very impulsively. His forte is his push. He lacks the serenity of discussion."[7]

As assistant secretary, Roosevelt was most concerned about the rise of Japan during the discussions about the annexation of Hawaii in 1897. He wrote to Mahan, "I am fully alive to the danger from Japan, and I know it is idle to rely on any sentimental good will towards us. . . . I have been getting matters in shape on the Pacific coast just as fast as I have been allowed. My own belief is that we should act instantly before the two new Japanese warships leave England. I would send the *Oregon*, and, if necessary, also the *Monterrey* . . . to Hawaii, and would hoist our flag over the island."[8] Roosevelt also warned Long about Japan: "Japan is steadily becoming a great naval power in the Pacific, where her fleet already surpasses ours in strength. . . . In my opinion, our Pacific fleet should constantly be kept above that of Japan."[9] As Roosevelt had warned, Japan positioned several naval ships, built in England and France, near Hawaii in an unsuccessful attempt to deter the United States from annexing the islands in 1897.[10]

At the same time, Roosevelt went overboard in response to the political rebellion in Cuba against Spanish rule. The Office of Naval Intelligence advocated an attack not only on Cuba but also on the Philippines to force a Spanish war indemnity and to tie down its Asian fleet. The Naval War College made plans for a defensive war off the U.S. coast if Britain joined Spain (never a possibility) or an attack against Spain itself if Britain stayed out. Typically, Roosevelt seemed open to all these options.

Privately, he referred to President McKinley as having the backbone of a chocolate éclair because of his caution around Hawaiian annexation and toward Spain in the Caribbean and the Philippines. In fact, the young and arrogant Roosevelt had much to learn from McKinley, who probably had as much direct battlefield experience as any American president, including driving a supply wagon through intense gunfire to save troops at Antietam. McKinley was also modest, a useful characteristic for a commander in chief. One Civil War comrade wrote to him after he was elected president, "I knew you as a soldier, as a congressman, as a governor, and now as president-elect. How shall I address you?" "Call me Major," McKinley replied. "I earned that. I am not so sure of the rest."[11]

Not surprisingly, an imprudent Roosevelt enthusiastically supported taking possession of the Philippines. No one, including Roosevelt, raised the issue of whether the United States could defend the islands from a rising Japan. In fact, the islands' vulnerability would constrain U.S. policy toward Japan, causing Washington to be less forceful than it might have been in its opposition to Japanese expansion during the 1930s and early 1940s. Moreover, Japanese war planners concluded that they would have to launch a war against the United States because the Philippines stood between Tokyo and Southeast Asia. Ironically, then, taking the Philippines made the United States more cautious and Japan more aggressive.

Roosevelt's unquestioning and enthusiastic support for taking the Philippines rounds out his early foreign policy career. His natural combativeness meant that he always supported the most assertive foreign policy and military options. Sometimes this made sense, notably when he pushed for the annexation of Hawaii and an expanded navy to protect it. However, more often than not he was guilty of excessive assertiveness, musing, for example, about taking Canada in 1895, and pushing hard to fight such an inoffensive European power as Spain in 1898 without asking whether a truly dangerous country might replace it, as Japan did in the Philippines and the Soviet Union in Cuba. He would come to regret this mistake.

Roosevelt as President

As president, Roosevelt discarded what remained of his blustery aggressiveness for several reasons. The weight of actual power upon becoming president after McKinley's assassination in 1901 at the age of forty-two had an impact; while still young, Roosevelt was no longer in his callow thirties.

International rivalries were also intensifying after the relative stability of the 1880s. Germany had adopted a more aggressive international policy after the firing of Bismarck in 1890. Russia was also expanding methodically across central Asia and into East Asia through the construction of railroads.

As a result, Britain began a major policy reorientation that Roosevelt noticed. In 1895 London backed off its tough stance over a border dispute between British Guiana and Venezuela after Washington sided with the latter. Shortly thereafter, Britain concluded that it could no longer contest American power in the Americas and used the Spanish-American War in 1898 as the fulcrum of the new policy. London sold coal and ships to the U.S. Navy, allowed Admiral George Dewey to communicate with Washington via the undersea cable in Hong Kong, opposed a European effort to organize support for Spain, and delayed passage of the Spanish fleet through the Suez Canal en route to Manila. The British fleet at Manila offered cooperation if the German naval vessels there threatened the United States. British foreign policy experts also told their U.S. colleagues that London and Washington had parallel interests in Asia, including preventing a possible Russian and German partition of China.

After the Spanish-American War, Roosevelt wrote to his friend Arthur Lee, the British military attaché in Washington, "I shall not forget, and I don't think our people will, England's attitude during the Spanish War, and we all know it saved us from a chance of very serious foreign complications." In a letter to another British friend in 1900 he hinted at the new special relationship, including a military alliance, which would blossom during most of the twentieth century: "There will always be at least a chance that in a great emergency, the nation of the two which vitally need it, may get more than moral aid from the other."[12]

Moreover, Roosevelt was no doubt pleased that the British had come to accept by 1899 a long-standing U.S. proposal that Washington be the dominant party in the construction of any future Central American canal, thereby modifying their equal status as stipulated by the 1850s Clayton-Bulwer Treaty.

Roosevelt's increasingly positive views on Britain were reflected in his attitude toward the Boer War (1899–1902). While he felt that American values favored the underdog Boers, he believed American interests lay with the British, and as someone who was now increasingly a geopolitical realist, he ranked the national interest as the highest of priorities. "If the British Empire suffers a serious disaster [in the Boer War]," he wrote to a British friend, "I believe in five years it will mean a war between us and one of the continental European military nations," no doubt referring to Germany.[13] He turned aside a delegation seeking humanitarian assistance to the Boers by asking where the United States should stop in providing such assistance—why not to the Danes under German rule or the Finns under Russian rule? And to his sister he wrote, "The trouble with the war is not that both sides are wrong, but that from their different standpoints both sides are right."[14] All were signs of Roosevelt's pursuit of a realist foreign policy, in which the national interest was paramount and the moral rights and wrongs were sometimes ambiguous and secondary.

In another sign of growing maturity, President Roosevelt took a relatively conciliatory approach to one of this first foreign policy challenges, the Alaskan boundary dispute in 1902. The dispute between the United States and Canada, which had developed with the discovery of gold in the 1880s, had come to a head. After Roosevelt concluded that he could no longer ignore the issue, he sent U.S. troops to the border as quietly and unostentatiously as possible. He also agreed to the British idea of an arbitration tribunal and rejected the more hawkish Lodge's advice to break off negotiations with London. A tribunal eventually ruled in America's favor, thereby removing a final obstacle to the growing U.S.-British rapprochement.[15]

As was the case with Britain, Roosevelt's attitude toward Germany evolved into a more nuanced point of view. From his early days, Roosevelt had taken a friendly but wary view of Germany. As noted, Roosevelt applauded the tough U.S. stance toward Germany on Samoa in 1889, but this incident came and went. In 1896, before becoming assistant secretary of the navy, Roosevelt wrote to a British friend recounting how the German ambassador to the United States, Hermann Speck von Sternberg, had spent several days at Roosevelt's home discussing a study that Berlin had asked him to do on the U.S.-German military balance in case of armed conflict. Roosevelt seemed more amused by the ambassador's "delightfully cold-blooded impartiality" than concerned about the German threat.[16]

As assistant secretary of the navy, however, Roosevelt mentioned periodically to friends his concern about German plans in the Americas: "I advocate . . . keeping our Navy at a pitch that will enable us to interfere promptly if Germany ventures to touch a foot of American soil. I would not go into the abstract rights or wrongs of it: I would simply say that we did not intend to have the Germans on this continent [i.e., the western hemisphere]."[17]

Roosevelt also objected to Germany's autocratic regime. As a republic, Germany could perhaps be a friend of the United States, but "under the present despotism she is much more bitterly and outspokenly hostile to us than is England." He criticized the kaiser's regime to a friend for running on about "imprisoning private citizens of all ages who do not speak of 'Majesty' with bated breath."[18] Roosevelt's dislike of autocratic Germany and Russia demonstrates that, unlike some critics who argue that political realists don't care about the domestic nature of international regimes, this American president did prefer democratic regimes to autocratic ones. At the same time, Roosevelt demonstrated his tough realist's frame of mind when he once wrote to a friend that if Germany wanted to expand it should attack Russia before the Slavic giant got too strong in order to carve out a buffer zone in central Europe, thereby leaving France, Britain, and the United States alone.

As president, Roosevelt's first diplomatic challenge involving Germany was the Venezuelan debt confrontation in 1902 and 1903, when Germany, Britain, and Italy bombarded Caracas briefly to force it to repay financial loans incurred during a recent civil war. London backed off its tough approach after it realized the damage this was doing to relations with Washington; Berlin, in its tone-deaf way, maintained a hard line. Roosevelt claimed, after he had left the presidency, that he had threatened the use of military force against Germany, something about which the historical record is unclear. What is certain, though, is that Roosevelt could see that Germany was the most aggressive party.[19]

Despite these concerns about Germany, Roosevelt regarded the European diplomatic and military balance as basically stable during his first administration. He knew that the German army was stronger than France's but also had to contend with France's ally, Russia, whose industrial strength was growing. In addition, while Britain was on a relative decline, it still had a strong navy. Roosevelt tried to reassure his friend Spring Rice about German intensions; Kaiser Wilhelm II was too jumpy and erratic to carry out any well-considered plans to attack Britain.[20]

However, Roosevelt became more concerned when Germany challenged France in Morocco early in his second administration. Roosevelt's role in the confrontation shows his ability to understand a complex diplomatic situation and to use guile to isolate the kaiser. The crisis originated when Germany challenged French plans to take charge of Morocco's deteriorating finances, including its ports, in coordination with Spain. Germany felt that it had a window of opportunity to challenge France because Russia, France's diplomatic and security partner since 1894, was losing a naval and ground war with Japan in 1904 and 1905.

Some members of the German government wanted to use the diplomatic incident as a pretext for hostilities. The chief of the German general staff, Count Alfred von Schlieffen, favored a preventive war against France because he felt that Germany's power position would erode over time against France and Russia, now that Britain had joined France in the Entente Cordiale in 1904. Baron Friedrich von Holstein, the regime's éminence grise, seemed to share this view and thought, at a minimum, that Berlin could shatter the French-British entente if London refused to back France over fear of being drawn into a war with Germany. The German chancellor, Prince Bernhard von Bülow, also hoped to shatter the new entente. Ironically, despite his blustery image, Wilhelm II was ambivalent about the Moroccan gambit. But his advisers and public opinion convinced him to insist on an international conference, opposed by France, to "solve" the Moroccan issue. The kaiser therefore landed with a German warship in Tangier in March 1905 and rode a white stallion around the city to underline his determination to oppose French-Spanish plans.

Back in Berlin, Wilhelm sent Roosevelt a message on June 11, 1905, urging him to use his influence with Britain to convince it to support the conference or stay out of impending French-German hostilities. At this point, Roosevelt intervened diplomatically with the French. On June 14 he met with French ambassador Jean-Jules Jesserand to urge French flexibility and promised to back France against unreasonable German demands. Roosevelt conveyed sympathy about the French predicament and confided to Jesserand that Wilhelm had asked him to intervene with the British, but that Roosevelt did not want to undermine the new entente by doing so. The next day France canceled all military leave, but its senior officers informed its civilian leaders that France would suffer a decisive defeat in case of hostilities. On June 19 Roosevelt cabled Paris, "What is needed is to give some satisfaction to the immeasurable vanity of William II."[21] On June 23 French prime minister Maurice Rouvier told Roosevelt via the French ambassador that Paris would agree to the president's suggestion because of its faith in his judgment and intentions. On July 1 a cowed France agreed to the conference.

The atmosphere remained tense as Germany called up its military reserves and France moved its forces to the German border just before the conference opened in January 1906 in Algeciras, Spain. The main issue was control of the main Moroccan ports by foreign police. Germany soon realized it could only count on Morocco and Austria-Hungary to support its position. Italy had a secret agreement with Paris over spheres of influence in North Africa despite its 1882 alliance with Berlin. Russia, Britain, and the United States backed France, despite Roosevelt's effusive flattery of Wilhelm. Roosevelt did not want Germany to control a single port in Morocco for fear that it would become a diplomatic and military foothold. While he supported French-Spanish police control over all the main ports, he cajoled the French into accepting Italy, Germany's two-faced partner, as a nominal inspector in charge of overall police administration as a sop to German pride. On February 17 France reluctantly accepted the U.S. compromise proposal.

On February 19 Roosevelt weighed in directly with the kaiser for the first time to break the impasse. He reassured Wilhelm that the Sultan of Morocco would be in charge of the organization of the police, even if he would be using French and Spanish police officers. The French and Spanish would report on an annual basis to Germany's supposed Italian ally. Germany, however, continued to reject the idea of French and Spanish police at all ports in favor of some German presence.

Roosevelt therefore went for the diplomatic jugular. Unbeknownst to Berlin, Ambassador Speck von Sternberg had gone beyond his diplomatic instructions in June 1905 by promising Roosevelt that Wilhelm would agree with all of Roosevelt's proposals at the conference. In fact, Berlin's instructions were that the kaiser would agree only to Roosevelt's proposals during the pre-conference negotiations between France and Germany. On March 7, 1906, Roosevelt cabled the kaiser with Sternberg's verbatim letter and reiterated the U.S. proposal that essentially backed the French position. Berlin was aghast over its ambassador's mistake but felt boxed in.

On March 18, Roosevelt went one step further and informed Berlin that he would have to publicly release the Sternberg letter in order to "clarify" the German position. Berlin reluctantly agreed to French-Spanish police control over all the ports, thereby bringing the conference to an end. Chancellor Bülow telegrammed Sternberg that "maintenance of the mutual trust between Berlin and Washington and immediate removal of all cause of misunderstanding are more important than the whole matter of Morocco." Roosevelt poured on the disingenuous flattery of Wilhelm's "epoch-making political success."[22] Guile had its place in Roosevelt's diplomacy.

Roosevelt Seeks to Balance Russia and Japan

Roosevelt also understood the diplomatic complexity of Asia, where the situation was even more multifaceted than in Europe. While Roosevelt had helped to support two status-quo powers in Europe, Britain and France, against a single expansionist country, Germany, he had to deal with two expansionist powers in Asia, Japan and Russia, with Germany lurking in the background.

During the 1890s, as noted, Roosevelt and U.S. foreign policy experts were most concerned in Asia about a rising Japan, which opposed the annexation of Hawaii. At the same time, however, Roosevelt's British and American friends were warning him about the challenge from Russia, which had been building railroads across central Asia during the second half of the nineteenth century. Spring Rice argued with him that Russia might attempt to expel Britain from India or to take control of parts of a weak China. Presciently, Roosevelt's friend Brooks Adams wrote in his book *America's Economic Supremacy* that Russia and Germany were benefiting from a declining Britain. Germany was the greater near-term threat because of its modern economy and military, but Russia, with its greater resources, posed the longer-term challenge. Mahan made similar arguments about an ascendant Russia weighing down on a declining Britain in Persia, India, and China in his book *The Problem of Asia*. The sooner the United States entered the geopolitical fray on the side of Britain to redress the deteriorating balance of power, the better, these friends advised Roosevelt.[23]

Initially Roosevelt was ambivalent regarding warnings about Russia. He felt that Russia did not threaten any immediate U.S. interests, though he agreed it could represent a serious longer-term challenge, "if not for our generation, at least to the generations which will succeed us."[24] However, Roosevelt identified a shorter-term challenge after Moscow took advantage of the unrest during the Boxer Rebellion to move about fifty thousand Russian troops into Manchuria in 1900 to protect its railroad construction crew and perhaps to incorporate the area into the Russian Empire, as it had been doing with much of central Asia. China, Japan, and Britain all protested the Russian move, to no avail. Roosevelt told his friends that he supported China's territorial integrity both as a general principle and as a way to avoid a partition that could exclude the United States. Moreover, Roosevelt feared that tensions between Moscow and Tokyo over China could drive apart Paris and London, their respective allies in Europe, where their cooperation was essential to contain Germany. At this point, Roosevelt's geopolitical analysis was as sophisticated as that of any other leader in the world.

Thus, Roosevelt began to tell confidants that Japan should oppose more forcefully the Russian presence in Manchuria. Perhaps Tokyo could now be a positive force in Asia rather than a negative one. If it had to expand, better it do so into the Asian mainland rather than the Pacific, where it could clash with the United States. With Roosevelt's tacit approval, Tokyo pushed without success for a Russian withdrawal from Manchuria during negotiations with Russia in 1902 and 1903.[25]

Anticipating a possible conflict, Roosevelt laid the groundwork for possible diplomatic mediation by contacting Japanese and Russian officials and carefully studying their motives and likely political and military goals in case of war. He learned ahead of time which ambassadors to bypass, including some of his own, and which to confide in.

Roosevelt was pleased at first with Japan's successful surprise naval attack in 1904 against the Russian Far Eastern fleet at Port Arthur, the port in southern Manchuria that Russia had leased from China. Interestingly, Roosevelt had anticipated Japan's military success at sea while most European countries, which the exception of France, assumed Russia would defeat a non-European power. Nor did Roosevelt criticize, even privately, the Japanese surprise attack; surprise attacks belong to the world of political realism, and Roosevelt was certainly a realist at this point.[26]

At the same time, Roosevelt did not want an overwhelming Japanese victory. Instead, he wrote to Lodge that he wanted a balance of power: "While Russia's triumph would have been a blow to civilization, her destruction as an eastern Asiatic power would also in my opinion be unfortunate. It is best that she should be left face to face with Japan so that each may have a moderative action on the other."[27] Similarly, he wrote to Spring Rice that no one should want Japan firmly established in China.

To this end, Roosevelt met in June 1904 at his home in Oyster Bay with Japanese Ambassador Kogoro Takahira and Baron Kentaro Kaneko, a Harvard graduate and envoy to the United States during the Russo-Japanese War. He told the two officials that Japan had a great future before it, but warned that "Japan might get the 'big head' and enter into a general career of insolence and aggression" and "such a career would undoubtedly be temporarily very unpleasant for the rest of the world, but that it would in the end be still more unpleasant for Japan." Roosevelt pointed to his policy of self-restraint in the Caribbean, where the United States had granted Cuba its independence and left the British and French West Indies alone. The two diplomats assured Roosevelt that "the upper and influential Japanese class" would not allow Japanese expansionism to happen. In light of future events, this was one of the most prophetic and poignant meetings in U.S. diplomatic history.[28]

Throughout 1904 Roosevelt told both parties that he would act as a mediator if they found that useful. Russia turned the offer aside because it wanted to recover from its initial defeats; Japan did likewise, thinking it could make further gains. At the same time, Roosevelt turned aside European powers' proposals for an international conference because he feared that Germany and France would gang up against Japan in a fruitless attempt to force it to give up its military gains. Japan was grateful for Roosevelt's opposition, a gratitude that Roosevelt would trade upon in his future mediation efforts.

Japan continued to make considerable progress in the war, and by early 1905 it had smashed the modest Russian Pacific fleet, taken Port Arthur after a long siege, and bested Russian ground forces in much of Manchuria. Japan's ground offensive culminated in its March victory at Mukden in southern Manchuria, the largest land battle of the war, where it inflicted about ninety thousand losses on Russia.

In addition to its previous demands to assume Russian rights to Port Arthur and the Manchurian railroad, Tokyo now insisted on a financial indemnity and rights to Sakhalin Island, north of Japan. Both parties had shared the large island during the nineteenth century until Japan ceded it to Russia in 1875. Japanese foreign minister Jutaro Komura, who had come to trust Roosevelt, told the U.S. president in the strictest confidence through Ambassador Takahira that he felt these new demands pushed by the Japanese military were excessive. Komura urged Roosevelt to intervene with the emperor to strengthen "the peace party."

Roosevelt held back for a short period, however. He told Lodge that the Russians would not accede to talks, let alone to the new demands, before the impending battle between the Russian Baltic Sea fleet en route to Asia and the Japanese navy. Sure enough, after the Japanese destroyed the Baltic fleet at the Battle of Tsushima in the Korean Strait in May 1905, the Russians reluctantly agreed to open negotiations under Roosevelt's auspices.[29]

Roosevelt's approach to the conference, which opened in August 1905 in Portsmouth, New Hampshire, demonstrated his mastery of diplomatic complexity. He did not approach the conference as a typical mediator who sought to be evenhanded. Instead, he pushed the Japanese demands on Russia for several reasons. First, Japan had generally bested Russia on land and even more at sea; Roosevelt felt that any peace settlement would have to reflect its military success to some degree. Second, he feared that Japan could continue to wage war and push Russia further out of Asia, thereby eliminating a check on Japanese power. Roosevelt was tougher on Russia because he did not want it to be weakened further. Third, he feared for the stability of the tsarist regime, which had faced violent political unrest beginning in January 1905. Fourth, he may have felt that in staying close to the Japanese during the initial negotiations, he would be in a better position to urge them to make the crucial compromises that would eventually be necessary.[30]

The conference deadlocked soon after it opened on August 9, with Japan demanding limits on future Russian naval forces in East Asia. Roosevelt convinced the Japanese to drop this demand; Sergei Witte, the head of the Russian delegation, noted dryly that this was not much of a concession since Japan had already sunk two of the three Russian fleets, the Pacific and Baltic, leaving only the Black Sea fleet intact. Russia agreed to give up most of its commercial concessions in Manchuria, including Port Arthur, to Japan. Both sides agreed to reduce their military forces in Manchuria. However, Russia refused Japan's insistence on the indemnity and on control of Sakhalin Island, much of which the Japanese had seized from Russia in July 1905. Roosevelt therefore proposed to Russia on August 18 that it offer to divide Sakhalin. Witte backed Roosevelt's proposal in a cable to the tsar: "If it is our desire that in the future America and Europe side with us, we must take Roosevelt's opinion into consideration." At the same time, Roosevelt urged diplomatic envoy Kaneko that Japan should drop the indemnity issue: "The sentiment of the civilized world . . . [would] back her [Russia] in refusing to pay." Roosevelt again wrote to Lodge about his concerns about a Russian collapse: "It is better that in the future, they [Russia and Japan] should both be strong enough to hold each other in check."[31] On August 29, the Emperor Meiji agreed to Roosevelt's urgings and instructed his government to abandon the indemnity demand in exchange for the southern half of Sakhalin Island. The Treaty of Portsmouth was signed on September 5.

Without Roosevelt's mediation, the two parties might have continued their war, though perhaps with a diminishing level of fighting in Manchuria. This might have endangered the Russian government's stability even if it did not result in a clear Russian military defeat. Instead, with both countries in the limelight, Roosevelt's international conference encouraged them to make hard decisions instead of putting them off indefinitely. All parties—notably the Russians and Japanese themselves—were laudatory, both privately and publicly, about Roosevelt's role in helping to bring the war to an end and for deservedly winning the United States' first Nobel Peace Prize.[32]

With Japan firmly established as the leading naval power in the western Pacific, Roosevelt acted with public respect, diplomatic accommodation, and subtle military threats. For example, he publicly criticized the California legislature's segregation of European and Japanese students and informed the Japanese that this did not represent the actions of the U.S. government in 1906.

Roosevelt also sought to accommodate Japan's rising power by not challenging its control of Korea and presence in southern Manchuria. Roosevelt subsequently explained his views in a letter to President William Taft in 1910:

> As I utterly disbelieve in the policy of bluff, in national and international affairs, or in any violation of the old frontier maxim, "Never draw unless you mean to shoot," I do not believe in our taking any position anywhere unless we can make good: and as regards Manchuria, if the Japanese choose to follow a course of conduct to which we are adverse, we cannot stop it unless we are prepared to go to war, and a successful war about Manchuria would require a fleet as good as that of England, plus an army as good as that of Germany.[33]

At the same time, Roosevelt sent the U.S. Navy's "Great White Fleet" (a reference to the color of the ships) around the world for the first time during his last year in office to send a signal about America's military power to Japan and to build public support for a high level of defense spending. He insisted that the visit be conducted with utmost courtesy but hoped that the spectacle of a three-mile line of modern battleships would have a sobering effect on Japanese expansionists.

Japan's welcome to the fleet and its gift of cherry trees to Washington several years later—a symbol of its wish for a relaxation of tensions—indicated that the message had been received. Roosevelt also ordered the fleet to visit Australia and New Zealand, the first implicit commitment by the United States to their defense.[34]

In contrast to the unanimous praise of Roosevelt's policies in Asia as well as in Europe, some observers have criticized President Roosevelt for an arrogant, imperialist policy toward Latin America. Yet his record is more complicated. Regarding the Panama Canal, Roosevelt's administration first negotiated a draft treaty with the Colombian embassy allowing the United States to pay for the right to build a canal across the Panamanian isthmus. It was only after the Colombian parliament rejected the draft treaty that Roosevelt supported independence for the province of Panama. Even then, he first sought a legal opinion to justify intervention based on an American treaty with Colombia of 1846. Privately, he told his advisers that he supported a political uprising in Panama, "but for me to say so publicly would amount to an instigation of a revolt, and therefore, I cannot say it."[35] When he sent naval ships to Panama to deter Colombian intervention, he did so without fanfare. Partly as a result, international reaction to the successful revolt was largely positive or neutral, even in Latin America; only in Germany did the press warn about the "master" expansionist.[36]

Moreover, Roosevelt pushed for an independent Panama because he felt the stakes were high and not from any general desire to throw U.S. weight around for its own sake. If the United States continued to maintain separate Atlantic and Pacific fleets, then it might suffer the same fate as Russia, which had taken months to bring its Baltic fleet to fight Japan. Significantly, the battleship U.S.S. *Oregon* took sixty-seven days to travel from San Francisco to the Battle of Santiago Bay in the Caribbean during the Spanish-American War. The trip would have taken about two and a half weeks if there had been a canal.

Roosevelt was also relatively cautious in his use of American power in the Caribbean. In 1902 he withdrew American forces from Cuba, as had been promised. In 1906 he initially turned aside requests for intervention from both opposing Cuban political factions, and he only agreed to send military forces after the Cuban government collapsed. He chose a civilian judge who never flew an American flag, rather than a military officer, to govern. Roosevelt withdrew American troops three years later after peaceful elections. He also turned aside the Dominican Republic's overtures for annexation in 1904: "I have about the same desire to annex it as a gorged boa constrictor might have to swallow a porcupine." Finally, at the 1907 Second Hague Conference, Roosevelt successfully pushed for the inclusion of all Latin American countries and championed an agreement barring the use of military force by advanced powers in collecting debts owed to them.[37]

One thing that all historians of Roosevelt agree upon is his strong interest in the country's military, specifically the navy. As president he succeeded with much effort in getting an average of two battleships a year authorized by Congress, in addition to many smaller vessels. He also descended in one of the navy's new submarines to the bottom of Long Island Sound, taking control of the vessel at one point. Roosevelt's idea of light entertainment was to sail out to the sound in his presidential yacht to analyze the target practice of the Atlantic Fleet.

Thus, as he welcomed home the U.S. Navy in 1909 just before leaving the presidency, Roosevelt could say to himself that three-quarters of the battleships that passed before his presidential yacht had been built during his administration. He had laid the groundwork for America's naval superiority in the twentieth century.

Roosevelt's Wilderness Years: World War I

Like many in the United States, Roosevelt was uncertain about who the guilty parties were in the outbreak of World War I (something historians still debate) and wondered whether perhaps a stalemate would be the best outcome, as had been the case with Russia and Japan. He also took a prophetic long view, writing to an English friend, "If Germany is smashed it is perfectly possible that later they will have to be supported as a bulwark against the Slav by the nations of Western Europe."[38]

This initial period of uncertainty ended quickly, however. As Germany drove deep into Russia and toward Paris, it became apparent that this was not a contest between roughly equal parties, but a war in which Germany could emerge as the European hegemonic power. Roosevelt was also appalled by the ruthless depredations of the German army, notably the destruction it wrought on Belgian and French cities, and the levy of a huge war indemnity against Belgium for defending itself: "To visit them with grinding punishment because of such action [defending their country] is proof positive that that any power which now or hereafter may be put in at the mercy of Germany will suffer."[39]

By the fall of 1914 Roosevelt and Senator Henry Cabot Lodge were criticizing President Woodrow Wilson publicly for standing aside from the existential struggle in Europe. Roosevelt viewed Wilson as an heir to the Democratic-Republicans who opposed a strong central government, including a robust military. He wrote to Lodge in December 1914 that Wilson and his secretary of state William Jennings Bryan were "worse than Jefferson and Madison." In January 1915 he wrote to the British foreign secretary that "pacifists" too often "drift helplessly into a war, which they have rendered inevitable, without the slightest idea they were doing so. . . . A century ago this was what happened to the United States under Presidents Jefferson and Madison."[40]

How fair was Roosevelt's criticism of Wilson? Some of it was excessive, as when he excoriated the president in private letters for being a physical coward. Wilson did convey a cerebral, academic quality—his physical exertion did not go much beyond throwing out a baseball on opening day of the season—but he was not a pacifist. Roosevelt was also perhaps too hard on Wilson for agonizing about the horrors of the European war. Wilson wrote perceptively about how the "mechanical slaughter" of the trenches had removed whatever glamour previous wars sometimes may have had in a 1916 memorandum after Verdun.[41]

Wilson's neutrality policy also reflected the views of most of the American public until Germany launched submarine warfare against all ships crossing the Atlantic in 1917. As Roosevelt wrote to a British friend in November 1916 about his support for U.S. military intervention, "My words carry no weight, and it would be unwise to pay any heed to what I said as representing the American people. . . . The Republicans by an overwhelming majority nominated [Charles Evans] Hughes precisely because he did *not* [Roosevelt's italics] represent my views" about the need to enter the war.[42]

Similarly, Roosevelt's and Lodge's assertive views also clashed with the constraints of public opinion after the United States entered the war. Both leaders wanted to drive deep into Germany to prove to the Germans that they should never again engage in a war against their European neighbors, especially those backed by the United States. If they had been heeded, perhaps even World War II would have been avoided. But here again, Roosevelt and Lodge would have failed to convince the American and European publics, who would have opposed the high price of casualties in an invasion of Germany.

However, Roosevelt's criticism of Wilson as a weak war leader, in the tradition of Jefferson, was more accurate in other areas. Roosevelt criticized Wilson for calling for the American public to be neutral "in thought as well as deed," whereas American interests and values argued for an Allied victory. Roosevelt also disliked Wilson's frequent harping on America's putative "unselfishness" and "disinterestedness." He found nothing wrong with reasonable self-interest; it was the way of the world and provided the foundation of any successful foreign policy. Roosevelt also considered that Wilson had no sense of personal or national honor. After the sinking of the *Lusitania* in May 1915, Wilson said Americans were "too proud to fight."[43] Roosevelt viewed Wilson's attitude as sanctimonious.

Roosevelt also felt that diplomatic negotiations would be dictated by military realities on the ground and that American troops would strengthen the president's hand as a negotiator, not weaken it. Just as Wilson was preparing a major mediation effort in early January 1917, the Germans declared war on all commercial shipping between the United States and Europe. The crucial U.S. contribution to the war effort did lead to military victory and to Germany's negotiated surrender, thereby proving Roosevelt's point.

The two presidents also differed in their vision of a postwar Europe. Wilson wanted a peace without victors, presumably because it might minimize any sense of revanchism in the losers. There was some truth to this point of view, but the best policy would have been a clear Allied victory, as advocated by Roosevelt and Lodge, followed by a magnanimous peace, as took place after World War II. Instead, the Allies did the opposite, a less than decisive victory followed by a harsh peace, which Wilson, to his credit, opposed at the Paris Peace Conference.

The two presidents differed most profoundly on postwar security measures. Roosevelt and Lodge were skeptical about Wilson's idea for a League of Nations that would enforce peace through its members' public opinion and a vague policing mechanism. Roosevelt wrote to several friends about his reservations, "I am for such a League provided we don't expect too much from it. . . . I am not willing to play the part which even Aesop held up to derision when he wrote of how the wolves and the sheep agreed to disarm, and how the sheep as a guarantee of good faith sent away the watchdogs, and were then forthwith eaten by the wolves." Similarly, he wrote to Senator Philander Knox of Pennsylvania in December 1918, "The League of Nations may do a little good, but the more pompous and the more it pretends to do, the less it will really accomplish." Roosevelt warned of those like Wilson who thought it possible "to secure peace without effort and safety without service and sacrifice. . . . In forming the league the chief danger will come from the enthusiastic persons who in their desire to realize the millennium at once, right off, play into the hands of the slippery politicians who are equally ready to make any promise when the time for keeping it is far distant."[44]

At other times, Roosevelt felt that the League of Nations could even be counterproductive. He wrote in January 1917, just before the United States entered the war, that a league could be premature and distracting; the first priority should be winning the European war. A league could also embroil the United States in disputes of only modest importance: "If his [Wilson's] words mean anything, they would mean that hereafter we intended to embark on a policy of violent meddling in every European quarrel. . . . Of course, as a matter of fact, the words mean nothing whatever."[45]

As an alternative, Roosevelt and Senator Lodge wanted an ongoing security partnership and a tacit alliance with Britain and France to dissuade Germany from launching another war. A number of leading British and French politicians, including French prime minister Georges Clemenceau, also held this view. So did a number of U.S. politicians, particularly Republicans from the East Coast. Unfortunately, they were distracted from the tacit alliance idea by the debate about Wilson's League of Nations. Roosevelt died in January 1919, so he did not engage in the debates and negotiations at the Paris Peace Conference. If he had, surely, he would have been skeptical of many of Wilson's idealistic ideas, notably the reliance on collective security and public opinion to deter aggressors.

Indeed, many European leaders shared Roosevelt's traditional views about the importance of a strong defense to maintain a stable balance of power. British prime minister David Lloyd George warned at the Versailles conference about the danger of surrounding Germany with independent states to the east that enjoyed the right of self-determination but would be vulnerable to a revanchist Germany. Clemenceau said publicly that he believed not in collective security, but in an effective balance of power in which Britain, France, and the United States would be stronger than Germany.

Historians believe that if Roosevelt had not died, he would have had a reasonably good chance of getting the Republican nomination and winning the election in 1920 at the age of sixty-two. And while even as charismatic a leader as Roosevelt would have had a difficult time rousing the nation from its isolationism, he would have pursued as vigorous and assertive a foreign policy as possible. He probably would have pursued a tacit security partnership with Britain and France, including resisting withdrawing U.S. forces from Europe in response to France's occupation of the Ruhr valley in 1923, as President Warren Harding did. No doubt he would have made major investments in cutting-edge weapons, notably aircraft, tanks, and aircraft carriers. Under his stewardship, the United States would have been better prepared to face the trials of the 1930s.

Roosevelt's foreign policy and his clashes with Wilson recall the early Federalist period, including its tensions between Washington and Hamilton and Jefferson and Madison. Both Washington and Roosevelt had to overcome their initial headstrong stubbornness and impulsiveness. Like Washington, who had to learn to pursue a less-than-heroic guerrilla war strategy, Roosevelt had to temper his combativeness with greater prudence. He came to believe that expansion for its own sake, as in the Spanish-American War, could be counterproductive. In fact, by 1907 he came to advocate independence for the Philippines, which he considered to be "the heel of Achilles."[46] He could still act boldly, however, in fostering Panamanian independence and in naval expansion, including sending the U.S. fleet around the world to remind Japan of American power.

During his presidency, Roosevelt repeatedly demonstrated his mastery of complexity. He was the first American president to realize that Germany constituted the main threat to peace in Europe, and he used a certain guile to cajole the kaiser into backing down from challenging France in Morocco. He was the first American president to believe that the United States had a vital interest in supporting the British and French democracies against Germany. But his subtle mind led him to believe that Russia could become the major long-term threat, thereby anticipating the Cold War era. In Asia, Roosevelt understood the Russo-Japanese relationship, which enabled him to play a useful mediation role and earned him the Nobel Peace Prize.

Roosevelt's differences with Wilson during World War I also illustrate the tensions between interests and ideals. Like Washington and Hamilton, Roosevelt believed in the traditional calculations of power, including the need to maintain a strong U.S. military. Just as Washington and Hamilton were skeptical about the Jeffersonian vision of a new diplomacy based on republican solidarity and economic sanctions, Roosevelt and Lodge objected to what they saw as Wilson's wishful belief in collective security and public opinion to prevent war. As president, Roosevelt took the United States to the edge of greatness; he might have taken it further if he had lived to be reelected.

CHAPTER 5

Franklin Delano Roosevelt

The Diplomacy of Guile

Franklin Delano Roosevelt resembled his cousin, Theodore, in several ways. Both were among the most cosmopolitan U.S. presidents, having spent considerable time in Europe as young men. Theodore could speak French and read German and Italian; Franklin spoke French and German. Each one served as assistant secretary of the navy, and both were intensely interested in world affairs. When Franklin had a chance to gain the nomination for governor of New York in 1918, he turned it down to remain in his position in the navy. Theodore wrote a highly regarded book on naval warfare in the War of 1812. Franklin read Alfred Thayer Mahan's *Influence of Sea Power on History* at the age of eleven; he enjoyed discussing naval history with Winston Churchill as president.

Like his cousin, FDR was flexible when important interests conflicted with ideals. He supported General Dwight Eisenhower's agreement with Admiral Jean-François Darlan, the commander in chief of Vichy forces, whereby French forces in North Africa would cease resistance in return for French North Africa remaining under Darlan's political control in November 1942. One of Roosevelt's aides, Samuel Rosenman, noted that Roosevelt "showed more resentment and more impatience with his critics throughout this period than at any other time I know about." When two of Charles de Gaulle's representatives protested the arrangement with Darlan in a White House meeting, Roosevelt lost his temper: "Of course I am dealing with Darlan," he shouted, "since Darlan's giving me Algiers! Tomorrow I'd deal with [French prime minister] Laval, if Laval were to offer me Paris!"[1]

Roosevelt also shared a certain Machiavellianism with his cousin, as well as with Washington and Lincoln. Theodore Roosevelt had flattered, cajoled, and subtly threatened the German kaiser during the Moroccan crisis; Washington had tried to keep the details of the controversial Jay Treaty secret from Congress; and Lincoln had applied the Emancipation Proclamation to the Confederate states but not to the slave states that remained in the Union.

Yet, Franklin Roosevelt was even more Machiavellian than his distinguished predecessors. Whereas they would use subterfuge on specific occasions, he resorted to guile as a standard procedure for four years (1937–1941) as he led the United States, however haltingly, toward World War II. He gave speeches that underlined his commitment to peace while educating the public about why war might be necessary. He worked with, against, and around Congress. He kept the country's extensive political and military cooperation with the British secret from the U.S. public after the fall of France. Sometimes he lied about it.

Unlike his more direct and impatient cousin, FDR could hide his feelings and intentions easily. He would often say yes to interlocutors, who assumed this meant agreement when it usually only meant that he understood what they meant. Sometimes, he would insert his own ideas into discussions with advisers in the guise of the ideas of others. He had a genial smile for all and called everyone by their first name, putting them at ease while conveying that he was in charge. He had many friends but no truly close ones.

As a proponent of an active U.S. role in world affairs and a strong defense, Roosevelt had to contend with the powerful peace movement that saw World War I as a huge mistake and felt that the United States should never engage in another war. Historians estimate that this isolationist movement, led principally by women's groups, clergymen, and students, had about 12 million adherents and an audience of about 50 million out of a population of 125 million by the mid-1930s. In 1931, the year Japan invaded Manchuria, twelve thousand clergymen signed a declaration opposing any future military engagements. In 1932 activists organized a mile-long automobile procession in Washington to present President Herbert Hoover with a "peace petition" signed by several hundred thousand Americans. In 1933 fifteen thousand students from sixty-five colleges pledged a commitment to either pacifism or to military service only in response to an invasion of the United States.

In addition to the mass peace movement, a smaller but still significant portion of the American public supported diplomatic initiatives and nebulous collective security measures to promote peace, but opposed any concrete military engagements. The smallest public opinion group supported strong measures to counter the rise of Germany, Italy, and Japan, even if this might result in war. Roosevelt belonged to this last group, but his public statements implied that he belonged to the first or second one.[2]

Although Roosevelt had to tread cautiously, given the strength of the peace movement, he had some room to maneuver with support for the navy because, as he said upon occasion, American mothers did not want their sons to be soldiers but they were willing perhaps to tolerate their sons being sailors. In 1933 he managed to obtain a threefold increase in naval funding in response to Japanese naval expansion, and to sell the buildup as a stimulus to the depressed economy. He told navy officials to play down the program publicly and to avoid criticizing those opposed to it. When hundreds of letters poured into the White House against the program, Roosevelt assured the public that the money would not be appropriated pending the results of the 1935 naval conference with Japan and Britain, which he said he hoped would lead to reductions in naval expenditures. In fact, Roosevelt instructed the U.S. delegation at the conference to make disarmament offers that he opposed but that he knew the Japanese would reject, thereby throwing the onus of failure onto Tokyo and allowing the naval construction to proceed.[3]

Ironically, the peace movement initially gained strength in response to the growing assertiveness of Germany, Italy, and Japan. In February 1935 Benito Mussolini sent additional troops to East Africa in preparation for the invasion of Ethiopia. In March 1935 Hitler publicly repudiated the disarmament clauses of the Versailles Treaty by proclaiming the existence of a German air force and plans to build an army of 550,000. Within a month, 50,000 veterans paraded through Washington, demonstrating against war on the eighteenth anniversary of America's entrance into World War I. On April 12,

1935, 175,000 college students staged a one-hour strike against war; thousands of students subsequently left their classrooms to demand "schools not battleships" and the abolition of the ROTC.

The same year, North Dakota senator Gerald Nye chaired a special investigatory committee that published a 1,400-page report blaming America's entry into the war on armament manufacturers and bankers. Walter Millis's best-selling book *Road to War: America 1914–1917*, popularized this thesis. As result of Nye's work and peace movement pressure, Congress passed three Neutrality Acts between 1935 and 1937. These laws prohibited all loans, financial assistance, and arms sales to countries at war. Purchases of nonmilitary goods for cash were allowed only if they were transported in non-U.S. ships. Roosevelt attempted to modify the laws to allow for some presidential flexibility, but he did not oppose them directly because he knew he would fail.

The strength of the peace movement and isolationism was reflected in America's reaction to the Italian invasion of Ethiopia in October 1935. Roosevelt, like most Americans, sympathized with the Ethiopians, particularly in light of Mussolini's thuggish son bragging publicly about the impact of Italian dive bombers. African Americans, who were beginning to vote Democratic in presidential elections, were particularly incensed; Haile Selassie was second only to Joe Louis in appearances on the front pages of the Black newspaper *The Chicago Defender*.

The peace movement was adamant that the United States should not cooperate with the League of Nations on economic sanctions against Italy. All Roosevelt could do was to call on U.S. businesses not to increase sales to Italy. In any case, the British and even more the French secretly backed away from an oil embargo against Italy for fear of pushing Mussolini closer to Germany. Italian forces entered Addis Ababa in 1936, and all discussion of economic sanctions ended. The West, including Roosevelt, had come across as feckless.[4]

During 1936 Roosevelt burnished his antiwar credentials in preparation for the national election. He gave his most vehement antiwar speech in Chautauqua, New York, on August 14, 1936: "I have seen war. . . . I have seen blood running from the wounded. I have seen men coughing out tear-gassed lungs. I have seen the dead in the mud. I hate war."[5] In the same speech he warned that if faced with a choice between peace and war profits, the United States must always choose peace. Roosevelt won every state except Maine and Vermont as a man of peace.

With the election behind him, Roosevelt took a more assertive stance toward international aggressors, including Japan, which had invaded the coastal areas of China in 1937. On October 5, 1937, he gave the so-called Quarantine Speech in Chicago, shortly after the Japanese atrocities in Nanking, China: "It seems to be unfortunately true that the epidemic of world lawlessness is spreading. When an epidemic of physical disease starts to spread, the community approves and joins in a quarantine of the patients in order to protect the health of the community against the spread of the disease."⁶ The speech was subsequently attacked by the isolationists, but this time Roosevelt did not entirely back away from it. At an off-the-record press conference, he simply said that that there were a number of things that could be tried and that he had an unspecified plan. He told Colonel Edward House, Wilson's foreign affairs adviser, that the country would slowly emerge from its isolationist shell.⁷

Roosevelt's growing assertiveness was reflected in his reaction to the destruction by Japanese planes of the gunboat U.S.S. *Panay*, which had been guarding American commercial vessels on the Yangtze River, on December 12, 1937. Roosevelt sent a tough note to Tokyo, demanding that the emperor be informed of his message. He asked his secretary of the treasury if he had the authority to impose economic sanctions on Japan—and what would happen if he did it without having that authority. On December 16 he told the British ambassador that he wanted "a systematic exchange of secret information" between American and British representatives, including plans for a blockade of Japan, which would be instituted after the next instance of Japanese aggression. However, public opinion was still clearly dovish, with many members of Congress demanding that all U.S. ships be withdrawn from areas of China-Japanese hostilities. The incident receded after Japan apologized and paid damages, but it was clear where Roosevelt's instincts lay.

The *Panay* incident was the first time that Roosevelt approached the British about military coordination in the event of armed hostilities. Roosevelt subsequently informed London that he was moving up the timing of U.S. naval maneuvers in the Pacific and would send several cruisers to Singapore for the opening of Britain's new naval base there. None of this was made public.[8]

American public opinion, however, remained deeply dovish. In January 1938 the House of Representatives nearly passed a constitutional amendment requiring a national referendum for declaring war except if the United States were invaded. Roosevelt had to make a personal appeal to prevent its passage. During the months leading up to the September 1938 Munich Conference, Roosevelt followed a somewhat contradictory path, reflecting the various pressures at play and his own ambivalence. He genuinely hoped that war would not erupt over Czechoslovakia and publicly and privately urged flexibility on the parties, which meant primarily that Prague should give way. Ever mindful of American public opinion, he denied a public statement in September 1938 by the American ambassador to France, William Bullitt, that France and the United States were united in war and peace. At the same time, he lamented to his cabinet that British prime minister Neville Chamberlain was for peace at any price and that Britain and France would "wash the blood from their Judas Iscariot hands."[9]

His meeting with British ambassador Ronald Lindsay on September 19, 1938, reflected his thinking. Asking Lindsay to keep their discussion from entering the public domain at all costs, Roosevelt warned that even if Britain and France succeeded in convincing Czechoslovakia to accede to "the most remorseless sacrifice ever demanded of a state," Hitler would continue his expansion into central Europe and probably to Denmark, Poland, or Romania.[10] Roosevelt, citing intelligence reports that Germany enjoyed military superiority, counseled Britain and France to avoid an attack against Germany that would probably lead to defeat. However, if Britain and France were to respond with a naval blockade of Germany, Roosevelt hoped he could persuade the American public to recognize the blockade and even send arms and munitions if there were no formal declaration of war.[11]

The issue became moot when the parties backed away from war at Munich on September 29, after the Czechs acceded to transferring the Sudetenland to Germany and to dismantling their fortresses. Roosevelt was relieved but believed that it was probably only an interlude before Hitler's next challenge.

After Munich, Roosevelt spoke out more often and more forcefully about the dangers to world peace and American security, and he took steps, for the first time, to support France and Britain militarily. Much of what he did he kept from the U.S. public and Congress, knowing that they would oppose it. Some of his acts bordered on illegality; not even his close aides were certain of his true intentions. Slowly, step by step, he led the U.S. public toward a war that he did not want but that he thought preferable to a German-dominated Europe.

Roosevelt approved a secret French mission to the United States to discuss purchases of American planes in October 1938. He first considered privately building parts in the United States and assembling the planes across the border in Canada to avoid the restrictions of the neutrality laws. The idea was too clever by half and never went anywhere. In December 1938 Roosevelt approved the sale of one thousand planes to France. Nonetheless, the military chiefs protested that the United States should not sell its most advanced planes because sensitive technology would no longer be under U.S. control and because the sale would inhibit the buildup of America's own inventory. They dragged their feet in showing the French the Douglas DB-7 attack bomber, as Roosevelt had ordered. On January 16, 1939, therefore, Roosevelt informed Secretary of War Harry Woodring that he wanted an all-out effort "to expedite the procurement of any type of planes desired by the French Government" despite Woodring's warning that the sale "might put the president in an embarrassing position."[12]

However, the secret French military mission to the United States was exposed when one of its members crashed in a test flight of the new A-20 light bomber at the Los Angeles municipal airport on January 23, 1939. Roosevelt hid his true motives by defending the sale for mainly commercial purposes. Discussions with the French proceeded openly, though production problems ended up slowing the number of U.S. planes that entered the French inventory in 1939 and 1940.[13]

Roosevelt's second military initiative after Munich, a major increase in U.S. aircraft production for the U.S. military, also ran into trouble from the parochialism of the military services. On November 14, 1938, Roosevelt told the army and navy joint chiefs that he wanted an air force of ten thousand planes and the ability to produce twenty thousand more a year. Army Chief of Staff General Malin Craig and Deputy Chief of Staff George Marshall argued that the United States needed a balanced increase of all forces, including ground forces and support staff for a large air force. Craig asked, "Who [are] you going to fight, what [are] you going to do with them, with three thousand miles of ocean?"[14] Roosevelt countered that producing a large number of planes might communicate to Hitler and Mussolini that the United States was serious about their aggression in the hopes of deterring further adventurism. Besides, while building up the army's manpower was politically impossible in the still-dovish atmosphere, increased aircraft production was less sensitive and could be sold as an economic stimulus.

In late December 1939 the president complained to his advisers about the military services' foot-dragging. He argued that he could not "influence Hitler with barracks, runways, and schools for mechanics." When his advisers asked what would happen if the planes were never used, Roosevelt answered that they could be given to the British. Roosevelt eventually acquiesced to the chiefs' arguments for a more "balanced" air force, but he had been right to place the discussion in the larger strategic picture instead of a narrow military one.[15]

During late 1938 and early 1939 Roosevelt tried to make the neutrality laws more flexible, but with little success due to the country's dovishness and because most of Congress assumed he would not run for reelection in 1940. Despite this setback, Roosevelt continued to try to educate the public and Congress about the dangers of international aggression and the need to modify the neutrality laws. In his State of the Union address in early January, Roosevelt named Germany, Italy, and Japan specifically for the first time as aggressors instead of just referring to aggressors generally. On January 31, 1939, he invited members of the Senate Military Affairs Committee, including isolationists such as Senator Nye, to the White House for an off-the-record discussion. Roosevelt spoke to them about his fears of Hitler's designs to dominate Europe and the importance of maintaining the Rhine as a barrier to German expansion. According to participants, Roosevelt said, "If the Rhine frontiers are threatened the rest of the world is, too."[16] Despite a pledge of secrecy, one or more of the senators relayed Roosevelt's comments to the press; an angry Roosevelt denied their accounts, thereby angering the isolationist senators even more.

To make Roosevelt's very point, German troops marched into Prague on March 15 to jeering Czech crowds, and Italy occupied Albania on April 7. As a result, American public opinion seemed to shift in favor of a revision of the Neutrality Acts to allow arms sales to Britain and France as long as the weapons were transported on non-U.S. vessels. However, members of the Senate and House foreign affairs committees still preferred to avoid revisions for fear of being forced into making a vote one way or another that would alienate parts of the electorate.

On April 15, 1939, Roosevelt sent a public message to Hitler and Mussolini asking that they give assurances that they would not attack thirty-one European countries and that they would agree to a disarmament conference that would include the United States. Hitler made fun of the proposal in a speech to the German parliament by reading the list of countries in a mock-bemused fashion, asking rhetorically which of these countries feared German attack and offering to guarantee their security—and even America's—if that would make everyone feel better. German parliamentarians reacted with hilarity. Roosevelt may have seemed naïve to European leaders, but he had again made his point to his target audience, the U.S. public, that Germany and Italy were the aggressors. Roosevelt may also have listened to Hitler's mocking response on the radio, since he would sometimes translate Hitler's speeches directly to his White House staff. The time for payback would come.[17]

In June the House Foreign Affairs Committee voted to allow sales of airplanes if they had civilian uses as well as military ones, but not to permit sales of military arms and munitions. On July 11 the Senate Foreign Relations Committee voted against even allowing this modification. Roosevelt fumed sarcastically to aides that Congress should pass legislation to erect statues of isolationist members in Berlin. On July 18 Roosevelt called a meeting with senior congressional leaders, including the isolationist Senator William Borah, in which he painted a grim view of the European situation. Borah denied that war was likely and almost got into a shouting match with Secretary of State Cordell Hull over congressional unwillingness to modify the Neutrality Acts. In early August 1939 Roosevelt predicted to staff that the war would break out on September 10; he would be off by ten days.

He was right again on August 4, when he sent a prophetic message to Soviet leaders that a Soviet-German pact would only delay an attack on the Soviet Union until after Germany had defeated France. After Moscow agreed to such a pact on August 22, Roosevelt continued to send messages to relevant parties, including the Italian king and Hitler, urging peace and flexibility. Even some of his aides felt this conveyed weakness and naiveté. This was true on one level, and someone like Theodore Roosevelt would never have sent them for those reasons. However, as noted, FDR's main audience was the U.S. public and his aim was to convince it that he had done everything he could for peace. Hence, there was a certain logic in his pleas, even if they made him seem ineffectual.[18]

Roosevelt told the nation in a radio address that the U.S. government would remain neutral with the declaration of war on September 1, but that "I cannot ask every American to remain neutral in thought."[19] He then called for a special session of Congress to discuss permitting the cash-and-carry modification of war supplies. This would allow friendly countries to buy U.S.-made military equipment and munitions from the private sector, but not from the U.S. armed services. The isolationists and peace lobbies, led by religious figures and activists such as Father Charles Coughlin and Charles Lindbergh, inundated Congress with thousands of telegrams, letters, and postcards. According to public opinion polls, they may have represented about one-quarter of the population. In contrast, more than 75 percent of Americans favored the Allies, of which about 50 to 60 percent favored military-related exports as long as they would not drag the country into war. On October 27 the Senate approved the cash-and-carry option by a vote of 63 to 30, and six days later the House voted 243 to 181 to do the same despite the peace lobbies.[20]

Despite the outbreak of hostilities in Europe, Roosevelt again faced the parochial attitudes of U.S. military leaders who did not want to permit the sale of any aircraft with sensitive technologies to Britain and France. Thus, in the spring of 1940, Roosevelt told Secretary of War Woodring and Air Corps Chief of Staff General Henry Arnold that he wanted the War Department to end its leaks to isolationist members of Congress to try to block such sales; offending officers would be punished, and Woodring should either cooperate or resign.[21]

However, the fall of France in June 1940 put a temporary stop to this trend toward greater support for Britain. Roosevelt, Congress, and the U.S. public first had to be convinced that Britain would continue to fight and that it would survive the coming German onslaught. No one wanted to send military equipment to London if it could end up in German hands, particularly when the United States would now have to spend more of its resources defending its own hemisphere against possible German attacks. Roosevelt told aide James Farley that he thought the chances of British survival were about one in three, and he signed the recommendations of his military planners on June 24 that commitments to sell London war matériel would only be made if London displayed the ability to survive a German assault. Churchill's desperate plea in late June for fifty to sixty American destroyers, given that Germany now dominated all of Europe and that German submarines were taking a heavy toll on British shipping, went unanswered.[22]

However, Churchill would demonstrate to Roosevelt and the world that Britain had the will to continue to struggle in an audacious decision. The German-French armistice of June 22 had left the French fleet, the second largest in Europe, completely intact and under the control of the Vichy government. Churchill's nightmare was that the Axis would take possession of the fleet through pressure on the French government or through an outright military takeover. He could not do anything about the French fleet at Toulon on the Mediterranean—40 percent of the entire fleet—because it was too well guarded by French naval and air defenses to attack. He did not have to worry about French vessels in England, in Alexandria, Egypt, and in the West Indies, all under British and American surveillance and constituting about 20 percent of the fleet. However, another 40 percent of the fleet was at ports in North Africa, particularly at Mers el-Kebir in Algeria, under Vichy control. Churchill therefore issued an ultimatum to French authorities: either sail the fleet in North Africa to the French Caribbean or the United Kingdom to join the war effort, or scuttle it. When French authorities refused these conditions, the British cabinet reluctantly came around to Churchill's plan, despite the appalling prospect of attacking a country that had been a military ally several weeks earlier.

Churchill had a second reason to press for military action. According to his principal private secretary, Eric Seal, Churchill "was convinced that the Americans were impressed by ruthlessness in dealing with a ruthless foe; and in his mind the American reaction to our attack on the French fleet was of the first importance."[23] Churchill was to keep Roosevelt informed about his plans, albeit with great discretion.

Ruthless the attack would have to be. On June 27 the British admiralty informed Vice Admiral James Somerville that he would attack and destroy the French fleet at Mers el-Kebir unless they scuttled or moved the fleet. He knew the attack would kill hundreds of French naval personnel, some of whom Somerville considered professional friends. On July 2 the admiralty sent the following message to Somerville, who was at Gibraltar: "You are charged with one of the most disagreeable and difficult tasks that a British admiral has ever been faced with, but we have complete confidence in you and rely on you to carry it out relentlessly."[24] Somerville assumed until the last moments that the French would give way to the British demands. On Churchill's orders, and apparently with Roosevelt's foreknowledge, the British attacked the French fleet on July 3, killing about 1,300 French sailors. Militarily, the attack was a mixed success. It destroyed much of the French fleet, but several of the most advanced ships slipped away. Politically, however, Roosevelt's aide Harry Hopkins told Britain's ambassador in Washington, Sir John Colville, that the attack had convinced Roosevelt that Britain was in the war for good.[25] Moreover, Britain demonstrated its staying power by holding its own during the aerial Battle of Britain that began around the same time.

As a result, Roosevelt cabled Churchill on August 13 that he would send fifty destroyers, twenty torpedo boats, and ten advanced aircraft. Since he did not have the legal right to give the equipment, according to Congress's restrictions, he proposed, and Britain accepted, that it would be "exchanged" for the sale or lease of British air and naval bases in the Western Hemisphere. The lend-lease proposal came at some political risk, given the approaching presidential election in November and the fact that the deal had been negotiated in secret. However, Congress was supportive given the impact of the fall of France and the British bases gambit, which FDR proclaimed with hyperbole as the greatest addition to U.S. defenses since the Louisiana Purchase.[26]

During August and September, FDR authorized the first exchanges between U.S. and British military officers and civilians of information and views about the aerial war against Germany, including British radar and U.S. preliminary plans for atomic weapons.[27]

Despite the approaching election, Roosevelt turned to the issue of conscription. In light of the German victory over France and

Britain's determination to fight on, public support for some form of military training for purposes of defending the Americas increased from about 50 percent to 65 percent. However, the peace lobbies were fiercely opposed to any form of training and congressional mail ran 90 percent against the idea. Nonetheless, Roosevelt came out publicly and forcefully in favor of conscription in August. In late August and early September, Congress narrowly voted in favor of the draft—to defend only the Americas—and gave Roosevelt the authority to use the National Guard for the same purpose.

After he won the 1940 November election, Roosevelt began taking greater risks to help the British, including bypassing the remaining Neutrality Acts. When Secretary of War Henry Stimson could find no way to declare the B-17 Flying Fortresses superfluous to the national defense, as stipulated by law, Roosevelt told him to release the planes to Britain to "test" them under combat conditions. When the U.S. Maritime Commission rejected the idea of building and leasing ships for which the United States had no demonstrable need, FDR told the British to purchase the ships directly from the shipyards and not through the U.S. government.

Despite these efforts, Churchill cabled Roosevelt in December 1940 that Britain needed more help. While the British had beaten back the prospect of a German land invasion by winning the Battle of Britain in the air, German submarines were ravaging British vessels crossing the Atlantic with food and war matériel from North America. Moreover, Britain only had about $2 billion to pay for $5 billion in military orders.

To avoid the Neutrality Act prohibitions on loans to belligerents, Roosevelt proposed the idea of a lend-lease bill that would allow him to provide military equipment to any country whose defense he considered vital to the defense of the United States. The military equipment would be repaid in kind after the war's end. At a December press conference he used the well-known analogy of one neighbor lending a garden hose to the neighbor next door whose house was on fire to prevent his own house catching fire.

To buttress his case, Roosevelt elaborated on his proposal during a fireside chat on December 29, declaring, "Never before since Jamestown and Plymouth Rock has our American civilization been in such danger. All of us, in all the Americas, would be living at the point of a gun—a gun loaded with explosive bullets economic as well as military. . . . To survive in such a world, we would have to convert ourselves into a militaristic power on the basis of a war economy. . . . Our national policy is not directed towards war. Its sole purpose is to keep war away from our country and our people. . . . We must be the great arsenal of democracy."[28]

During this same period he authorized secret discussions in Washington for the first time between U.S. and British military officers to discuss not just intelligence issues pertaining to the war but also the coordination of military operations, should the United States enter the war. In January 1941 he told the press that he did not want the U.S. Navy to escort merchant ships because it might draw the United States into the war, even though he knew American and British officers were discussing this military operation.[29]

Once Congress passed Lend-Lease in March, 60 to 31 in the Senate and 317 to 71 in the House, including the provision allowing the president to decide which countries would be included, Roosevelt moved immediately. He directed the armed services to send half of their production of new weapons and munition to Britain, agreed to repair British vessels in American shipyards, and seized sixty-five German, Italian, and Danish ships detained in U.S. ports for use by the British and the United States. He also took advantage of British victories over Italian forces in East Africa to declare the Red Sea region no longer a combat zone, which allowed American merchant ships to carry supplies to British forces in the Middle East, thereby releasing British merchant ships for the dangerous Atlantic Ocean crossing. He concluded an agreement with the Danish ambassador in Washington to place Greenland under U.S. protection, thereby permitting the construction of military bases there.[30]

Despite these steps, the major problem facing Britain remained the actual transport of supplies from North America to Britain in light of the mounting toll of German submarine attacks. By the first months of 1941, Germany was sinking British merchant ships at least three times faster than London's annual capacity to replace them. At some point there would be no ships to transport food, military equipment, and munitions from North America. According to the

Neutrality Acts, U.S. merchant ships could not carry goods to Britain. Roosevelt had also forbidden U.S. Navy ships from escorting British and foreign ships between North America and Britain, a position supported by the American public by 50 to 41 percent.

Roosevelt therefore informed Churchill in the strictest secrecy that he would not authorize U.S. Navy escorts for convoys, but he would provide more extensive patrolling. U.S. aircraft and naval vessels would now search for German submarines and inform British convoys of their whereabouts as far out as Greenland, the Azores, and halfway between Brazil and West Africa in the South Atlantic. The United States would use bases in Canada, Greenland, Bermuda, the West Indies, and Brazil if possible, as well as the United States. In effect, the United States was at war with Germany on the sea.[31]

In May Roosevelt told his senior advisers he wanted to move a quarter of the Pacific Fleet to the Atlantic to support the British. Secretary of War Stimson supported the proposal because the Atlantic and Europe were his priority and he wanted to make the move public to boost British morale. Secretary of State Hull opposed the proposal because he was in charge of negotiations with Japan and wanted to keep any move secret to avoid emboldening Japan. Roosevelt sided with Stimson on both counts.[32]

That same month, unbeknownst to the U.S. public, Roosevelt authorized American military personnel to train British pilots in the United States. American military personnel were also copiloting British reconnaissance planes over the Atlantic, including the aircraft that located the *Bismarck*. When the navy phoned the news of the *Bismarck*'s sinking to the White House, the president shouted to his two speechwriters, Robert Sherwood and Samuel Rosenman, "She's sunk." Rosenman later commented, "There could not have been more satisfaction in his voice if he himself had fired the torpedo that sank her."[33]

While the United States was now at war with Germany in the Atlantic, Roosevelt told the cabinet that he did not want to take the country into war formally unless there was a serious clash initiated by the Germans: "I am not willing to fire the first shot." If Germany began hostilities, then Americans would be united. Roosevelt therefore did not order military retaliation when a German submarine sunk an American freighter, the *Robin Moor*, in the South Atlantic on June 11.[34]

In July he sent a marine brigade of four thousand nonconscripts to Iceland to free up the twenty thousand British military personnel there and to forestall reported German plans to take the Danish territory. Churchill's conviction that it would have an important impact on British morale probably also played a part in the decision. However, Roosevelt still did not have the legal authority to send conscripts outside of the Western Hemisphere to Iceland, as the British and Icelanders urged upon him.

On July 14 congressional leaders promised reluctant support for extending draftee service from one year to eighteen months, but not for a more indefinite "state of emergency" period. However, they insisted that a proposal giving Roosevelt the authority to send draftees outside the Western Hemisphere be deferred. Despite the president's extensive lobbying, the entire Senate approved the service extension to eighteen months by only a modest margin and the House did so only by a single vote in August. A congressional staffer commented that he had never seen such fear of a bill in forty years on the Hill.[35]

On August 9 Roosevelt and Churchill met for the first time at the Atlantic Conference in Placentia Bay off Newfoundland. In typical fashion, Roosevelt insisted that the meeting be kept secret until he could announce its broad principles, the Atlantic Charter, at the meeting's conclusion. Both men were delighted to meet each other. Churchill was a legend going back to his cavalry charge in the Sudan in 1898, and Roosevelt represented potential salvation for Britain. Hopkins, who accompanied Churchill from Britain, described the scene this way: "You'd have thought he was being carried up into the heavens to meet God."[36]

While both men got on well, they were disappointed in the conference for different reasons. Churchill had hoped for a U.S. declaration of war, but Roosevelt would only promise greater U.S. military support. He told Churchill the U.S. Navy would now protect convoys—including British merchant ships—in most of the Atlantic, drawing a line on a map running from east of the Azores to east of Iceland. As Churchill reported to the cabinet:

> The President's orders to these escorts were to attack any U-boat, which showed itself, even if it were 200, or 300 miles away from the convoy. . . . Everything was to be done to force an "incident."

This would put the enemy in the dilemma that either he could attack the convoys, in which case his U-boats would be attacked by American naval forces, or, if he refrained from attack, this would be tantamount to giving us victory in the Battle of the Atlantic. . . . The President . . . made it clear that he could look for an "incident" which would justify him in opening hostilities.[37]

Roosevelt, for his part, was disappointed that the conference did not have much impact on an ambivalent American public, despite the Atlantic Charter principles and the stirring Sunday service when service members from both countries sang "Onward, Christian Soldiers" on the H.M.S. *Prince of Wales*. Polling showed that three-quarters of the U.S. public still wanted to stay out of the war.

Despite these dovish polls, Roosevelt began using every incident with the Germans in the Atlantic as a means to engage in greater hostilities. On September 4 a British reconnaissance plane spotted a German submarine in the North Atlantic and informed the nearby U.S. destroyer *Greer*. Both plane and vessel attacked the submarine with bombs and depth charges, but without success. The submarine fired several torpedoes that missed the *Greer*. The navy reported to the White House that there was evidence that the submarine knew the nationality of the *Greer,* though other intelligence reports indicated that Hitler wanted to avoid attacking American vessels.

In any case, Roosevelt used the incident to announce his new policy in a radio address two days later. He told listeners that the submarine had fired first on the *Greer*, which was not true:

It is time for all Americans to stop being deluded by the romantic notion that the Americas can go on living happily and peacefully in a Nazi-dominated world. . . . This [attack] was one determined step toward creating a permanent world system based on force, on terror, and on murder. . . . When you see a rattlesnake positioned to strike, you do not wait until he has struck before you crush him. These Nazi submarines and raiders are the rattlesnakes of the Atlantic. . . . Our patrolling vessels and planes will protect all merchant ships—not only American ships but ships of any flag—engaged in commerce in our defensive waters. . . . Let this warning be clear. From now on, if German and Italian vessels of war enter the waters, the protection of which is necessary for American defense, they do so at their own peril.[38]

Framed in these dramatic terms, the "shoot on sight" policy applied to the large expanse between the United States and Iceland gained the approval of 62 percent of the U.S. public.

On October 16 a German submarine attacked the destroyer *Kearny* on convoy duty near Iceland, killing eleven American seamen. Roosevelt won approval to arm U.S. merchant ships the following day by two votes to one in the House of Representatives, though they still stopped at Iceland. On October 31 a German submarine attacked the destroyer *Reuben James* on convoy duty near Iceland, killing 115 sailors. Roosevelt announced—falsely—that he had come into possession of secret Nazi documents revealing plans to divide Latin America into five vassal states and abolish all religion. He obtained congressional authorization to send Lend-Lease goods on American merchant ships in U.S. naval convoys beyond Iceland to Britain itself. This period of subterfuge finally came to an end with the Japanese attack on Pearl Harbor on December 7 and the subsequent German declaration of war against the United States.

Roosevelt's diplomacy illustrates a number of principles for effective statecraft. As mentioned, he could be flexible about moral compromises if they advanced the war effort, as they did in American dealings with Vichy French officials. Roosevelt also wisely overrode his senior military advisers, who wanted to invade France in 1942 or 1943, and came down on the side of Churchill, who wanted to gain first air and sea superiority in the Atlantic area. In doing so he matched ends and means effectively. Roosevelt could also support audacious uses of military power, as he did when backing Churchill's attack on the French fleet in North Africa in 1940.

What is most striking about Roosevelt's diplomacy during the prewar period was his constant need to hide his true intentions. For four long years he pushed the U.S. Congress and public toward assisting the Allies without creating an isolationist backlash. Other, more direct leaders, such as Alexander Hamilton and Theodore Roosevelt, would have found his strategy of guile maddening. However, Franklin Roosevelt had the temperament and discipline to hide his true feelings and intentions. But it still must have been hard—even for a man who had drawn on deep inner resources to battle polio for years. Eleanor Roosevelt noted that after the attack on Pearl Harbor, she had never seen him so serene. Guile had had its pride of place in his prewar diplomacy, but now it would give way to the grinding determination required in war. He delivered his declaration-of-war speech to Congress and the nation with controlled fury.

CHAPTER 6

Truman and Acheson in the Korean War

When Reasonable Leaders Stumble into Disaster

Our previous chapters have dealt with political leaders who displayed a true mastery of statecraft, even though they made mistakes, especially in their early years. One characteristic they shared was the ability to stand back from a given situation, sometimes fraught with emotions, and make a judgment that went against the dominant view at the time. Unlike most Americans, Washington and Hamilton were not swept up in the initial pro–French Revolution feeling and supported the unpopular Jay Treaty with Britain. Lincoln and Seward ignored the initial widespread public outrage against Britain during the 1861 *Trent* affair. Theodore Roosevelt, unlike most observers, thought that Japan would defeat Russia in 1904. Franklin Roosevelt worked with Vichy France officials in North Africa, despite hostile U.S. public opinion. In contrast, President Harry Truman and his distinguished advisers, Secretary of State Dean Acheson and Secretary of Defense George Marshall, despite their major accomplishments, allowed the immediate emotional atmosphere to dominate their decision-making at several key moments during the Korean War.

Truman, Acheson, and Marshall were reasonable men, not given to the excessive stubbornness of the young Washington, the impetuousness of the young Theodore Roosevelt, or the ambivalence about power of Jefferson. Yet reasonable leaders at times make blunders because they do not think through key policy challenges rigorously. Some of their advisers did analyze these challenges with more discernment, but their advice was not heeded. For the purposes of our study on statecraft, then, let us turn to the initial mistakes surrounding the Korean War as good illustrations of reasonable leaders who nonetheless committed grievous policy errors.

At the same time, let us not forget that President Truman made a courageous decision to oppose North Korea's invasion. In doing so, he salvaged the southern half of Korea from the nightmare of communist North Korean rule and made possible the transformation of the impoverished southern part of Korea into a successful democracy and one of the world's leading economies.

The mistakes of 1950 had their origins in the immediate postwar period. Korea was not a high priority for the victors at the end of World War II. Senior U.S. and Soviet leaders were not involved in the decision to divide the country temporarily at the 38th parallel in order to oversee the Japanese surrender. By luck, the United States' sector turned out to contain most of the Korean population.

This Soviet-U.S. comity did not last long. An intense rivalry soon broke out between the communist government in the north under Kim Il-Sung and the noncommunists in the south under Syngman Rhee, who had fled Japanese rule to live in the United States in 1910. Both leaders were single-mindedly determined to unite Korea under their respective control; they would brook no compromise and launched guerrilla raids into each other's territory. At the same time, Soviet and American officials in Korea began to disagree even on simple administrative issues, reflecting the coming Cold War atmosphere.

Nor were the Americans sure of what they really wanted in Korea and how much they were willing to do to achieve it. The State Department wanted to maintain a pluralistic South Korea as part of an incipient anti-communist policy in East Asia, including shielding Japan from communist influence emanating from the Korean peninsula. President Truman largely shared this view but was not willing to pay for the resources to back it up.[1]

In fact, the Defense Department recommended withdrawing its forty-five thousand occupying military personnel in part in response to pressure from Truman, Defense Secretary Louis Johnson, and parts of Congress to reduce the defense budget. Moreover, growing tensions in Europe caused the Defense Department to focus on a pos-sible Soviet attack there. Other priority targets, it was thought, were the U.S. homeland or perhaps Turkey and Iran, where there had been confrontations in the late 1940s.

The Pentagon's fear of a Soviet attack in Europe or the United States represented unrealistic worst-case scenarios, another trap to be avoided for effective statecraft. The United States enjoyed a superior nuclear inventory during the early Cold War, and the Soviets did not have ballistic missiles with nuclear weapons to reach the continental United States until the mid- or late 1950s. In any case, the Soviets were hardly willing to hazard another world war after losing 10 per-cent of their population in the conflict with Germany.[2]

Given the Defense Department's fears about a Soviet attack out-side of Korea, the Pentagon saw an opportunity to end the Korean commitment when the Soviets proposed a mutual U.S.-Soviet with-drawal in 1947. That September, the joint chiefs, including General Dwight Eisenhower, sent a memo to Secretary of State Acheson, who showed it to Truman, which argued that Korea was not important from the standpoint of military security. The memo therefore recom-mended that the United States pursue a Soviet proposal for a mutual military withdrawal. The memo posited, but rejected, the option of U.S. forces remaining in Korea in the event of a Soviet withdrawal be-cause this would be unacceptable to the American public and would subject the United States to international censure, which turned out not to be true. The Pentagon also indulged in excessive optimism about its ability to handle any North Korean threat to South Korea with its air forces in Japan.[3]

Truman mentions in his memoirs that the mutual withdrawal proposal struck a chord with him because he remembered his grand-parents complaining about the Northern occupation of his state of Missouri after the American Civil War. Truman failed to realize, how-ever, that the Cold War situation was different: South Korea, faced with a deadly North Korean military threat within artillery range of its cities, wanted an indeterminate U.S. military presence. Secretary of State Acheson and U.S. Ambassador to South Korea John Muccio, for their parts, also supported the mutual withdrawal proposal.[4]

One of the few lonely voices raised against a withdrawal of U.S. combat troops belonged to Deputy Undersecretary Dean Rusk, the future secretary of state under Presidents John F. Kennedy and Lyndon Johnson. Rusk thought it would increase the chances of a communist attack. Hawkish by nature, he would turn out to be as right about Korea as he would be wrong about the Vietnam War.[5]

Soviet combat forces left North Korea by December 1948; U.S. combat forces departed from South Korea by June 1949. In the meantime, Truman and Acheson lobbied with only mixed success for robust economic assistance and military funding for a U.S. military training mission of seven thousand soldiers remaining in South Korea. Many inward-looking congressional members echoed the Pentagon's lack of interest.

Truman's case for continued support was not made easier by the vocal right-wing China lobby, which opposed helping South Korea unless the United States helped Chiang Kai-shek to defend Taiwan against a likely Chinese attack. Truman and Acheson opposed this because it would eliminate any hope of keeping China out of the Soviet orbit; the Defense Department opposed it because it would force the United States to focus too much on East Asia. Thus, to be fair to President Truman and his advisers, even if the administration had wanted to make an explicit public commitment to defend South Korea, it would have run into considerable congressional opposition. Acheson succinctly characterized the situation in a letter, writing, "The all-or-nothing boys refuse to do what is possible in Korea, because we will not attempt what is impossible in China."[6]

Unfortunately, communist leaders misread the U.S. withdrawal from Korea and congressional criticism of assistance to South Korea as signs of a total lack of interest in Korea, whereas it represented more a general uncertainty. The seeming indifference would change in a heartbeat with the brazen North Korea invasion, thereby showing once more that in the heat of conflict, emotions are volatile.

The Truman administration compounded this misimpression with several misleading major speeches. In March 1949 General Douglas MacArthur stated that the United States would defend Japan and the Philippines but excluded South Korea from the U.S. defense perimeter. Ironically, in light of later events, the then-dovish MacArthur said privately that the United States was not capable of providing adequate training to the South Koreans to defend against an attack by North Korea.[7]

Acheson also excluded South Korea from the defense perimeter in his press club speech on January 1950, though he warned potential aggressors that their victims could rely "upon the commitments of the entire civilized world under the Charter of the United Nations."[8] The problem with this Wilsonian rhetoric was that these commitments were highly uncertain and the Soviets could veto UN resolutions. To the communist side, the speech may well have sounded like empty sloganeering, even though it did not turn out to be.

Tellingly, Acheson's reference to South Korea made little impact in the U.S. press because journalists focused on his remarks about China. In addition, like the Defense Department, Acheson was spending most of his time on Europe and the creation of NATO. South Korea was still something of an afterthought in early 1950. America's burgeoning global commitments meant even important issues could fall through the cracks.[9]

The Acheson speech with its somewhat ambiguous reference to Korea reflected the uncertainty of U.S. policy. Never, according to the memoirs of Truman and Acheson, did Truman and his advisers ever sit down to think about what they would do if North Korea invaded the south. They had other priorities and never thought it would come to that. At worst, in their expectation, continued North Korean guerrilla attacks and social unrest in South Korea could undermine the regime and perhaps even bring it down in stages.[10]

Were senior U.S. officials, including Truman, the victims of shoddy intelligence? Yes and no. The CIA consistently warned that the USSR could permit North Korea to try to overrun the peninsula as the United States and Soviet Union withdrew their military forces and that the Chinese communists could turn their attention to Korea following their victory. In 1949 the CIA stated that a continued U.S. military presence would help to deter a North Korean invasion and provide stability and self-confidence to the South Koreans. Significantly, the Departments of State, Navy, and Air Force concurred with this assessment, though army intelligence downplayed the North Korean threat, reflecting the army's desire to leave Korea.

Granted, the CIA did not forecast the June 1950 invasion despite the evidence of North Korean and Chinese military buildups. Intelligence analysts probably assumed that the buildups were defensive responses to Rhee's belligerent public threats to invade the north—a main reason for the limitations on the amount and quality of arms that the United States provided to him. Thus, the CIA in 1950 had warned senior officials about the possibility of a North Korean invasion, albeit in general terms.[11]

Could the Korean War have been avoided if the Truman administration had been more forceful in its commitment to South Korea? According to Soviet and Chinese archives opened during the 1990s, Premier Kim had been pushing Joseph Stalin and Mao Zedong vigorously beginning in 1948 to allow him to conquer the South. Stalin and Mao were initially cautious and only gradually came around to approving an invasion in early 1950. Even then, they were always wary of U.S. military intervention. A more categorical U.S. promise to defend South Korea could have dissuaded Moscow and Beijing from backing Kim's gamble.

Could the Truman administration have made such a commitment, given the significant—but not overwhelming—opposition to defending South Korea in Congress and the Defense Department? Yes—if Truman and Acheson had resorted to the guile of a Franklin Roosevelt. Specifically, they could have told Soviet leaders privately and Chinese leaders via third parties that they would intervene militarily in case of an invasion. They could have kept a small number of ground and air combat units, in addition to military trainers, in the south on a rotating basis as a deterrent. The Korean War might have been avoidable if the United States had shunned the muddle of the middle path and determined that it would fight to defend South Korea. For effective statecraft, knowing one's own intentions is often as important as understanding those of adversaries.

Nearly all the indifference and ambivalence about South Korea's fate disappeared with the North Korean invasion on June 25. As mentioned, Acheson and others at State had always felt that concrete interests were at stake; now the Defense Department saw an opportunity to get rid of the communist threat in Korea once and for all. The congressional China lobby also saw Korea in a new light, as a back door to defeat the Chinese communists and help Chiang return to the mainland via Korea.

Truman's response, as well as that of others, was visceral: communist thugs were not going to brazenly push the United States out of Korea. Truman recounts in his memoirs that the invasion recalled the

Japanese invasion of Manchuria in 1931, the first step toward World War II. Truman and the U.S. government incorrectly assumed that the Soviets had driven the decision to invade and that it could be a first step in a wider Soviet military campaign. He also knew that Republicans were ready to pounce if Truman "lost" another country to communism.[12]

Truman had great respect for Acheson, the brilliant and experienced, if acerbic, adviser he had appointed secretary of state in January 1949. He had a good rapport with his secretary of defense from 1950 to 1951, George Marshall, who had been chief of staff of the army during World War II and secretary of state before moving to the Pentagon. If there was a weakness here, it was due to Truman and Acheson sometimes deferring too much to Marshall because of his World War II prestige. And Marshall, a military man, tended to defer to the commander in the field, the headstrong MacArthur.

MacArthur was not a reasonable pragmatist like Truman, Acheson, and Marshall. His brilliant military record in World Wars I and II was matched only by his vanity, willfulness, grandiosity, and recklessness. Truman had always considered him to be a stuffed shirt; Acheson said dealing with MacArthur was like dealing with a foreign power. General Omar Bradley once told MacArthur that he had a court, not a staff. Yet MacArthur had strong ties with conservative congressional Republicans, some of whom had promoted him to be a presidential candidate in the 1944 election, in which he won several states. Truman and Acheson knew they would pay a price in Congress for crossing the well-connected general.

How did America's adversaries, Stalin and Mao, see the war? If Truman, and even more the U.S. military, saw the invasion through a worst-case-scenario lens of a first Soviet step in a larger military campaign, Stalin and Mao saw it through somewhat rose-tinted lenses. They thought that the United States probably would not react militarily, given its other global preoccupations and its seeming indifference to Korea. Still they did not completely rule out that possibility. The more reckless and self-serving Kim assured them that North Korea would win in several weeks before the United States had time to react.

What Stalin and Mao failed to understand was that Truman and his advisers were no longer evaluating the stakes in Korea as a theoretical matter, but making decisions in front of the entire world. The

American leaders felt that U.S. credibility was on the line, and that they were not going to be made fools of by a minor communist power. The determination of Truman and his advisers to fight underscores that major decisions, especially those made during a crisis, are not always cool and cerebral; they are often driven by intense emotions in addition to domestic politics and the perceived national interest.

The Soviets made another blunder by continuing to boycott UN Security Council meetings over the American unwillingness to admit China to the United Nations. This allowed the council to avoid a Soviet veto and to vote 9 to 0 in favor of a North Korean withdrawal behind the 38th parallel. UN approval would facilitate U.S. policy domestically by giving it a patina of international approval. Moreover, a number of UN members would send troops to South Korea, although the more effective nations, Britain, France, and Turkey, probably would have done so even without UN sanction. In contrast, UN criticism of North Korea had no impact on Soviet, Chinese, and North Korean thinking. The Wilsonian dream of an effective international body had once again come up short. The reality was closer to Theodore Roosevelt's view that the league might play a modest role but could not be relied on to deal with major challenges.

Truman initially demonstrated an impressive ability to balance forcefulness and a sense of limits during the first days of the war. On June 26, 1950, at Acheson's recommendation, he ordered U.S. air and naval units into action, but only south of the 38th parallel. On June 27, with the fall of Seoul, he authorized MacArthur to launch airstrikes against airfields and ammunition and fuel dumps in North Korea. However, he refused the Defense Department's recommendations to remove all restrictions on MacArthur's actions. He told the National Security Council on June 29, "We want to take any steps we have to push the North Koreans behind the line, but I don't want to get us overcommitted to a whole lot of other things that would mean war. . . . MacArthur is not to go north of the 38th parallel." On June 30 Truman ordered U.S. ground troops performing occupational duties in Japan to South Korea at MacArthur's urging.[13]

At the same time, Truman made several momentous decisions without realizing their true ramifications. At Acheson's recommendation, he sent the Seventh Fleet to guard Taiwan against a Chinese attack and to prevent Taiwanese guerrilla raids against the mainland.

He also significantly increased military assistance to France in Vietnam, the first serious U.S. commitment there. Without meaning to, these actions probably strengthened China's already strong anti-American views, thereby increasing the chances of Chinese military intervention in Korea.

In July the newly arrived American military units from Japan slowed but did not stop the North Korean advance. U.S. ground troops were outnumbered, and most had only experienced undemanding occupational duties in Japan. Antiquated bazooka rounds bouncing off T-34 tanks epitomized the unpreparedness of the first American troops. However, during August the Americans and South Koreans stabilized a precarious retreat; they managed to control a box some seventy-five by forty miles of land around the South Korean port of Pusan, less than 20 percent of South Korean territory.[14]

With the stabilization of the military front, senior officials debated U.S. policy goals and strategy. Hawks in the State Department's Far East Bureau, represented by Assistant Secretary Dean Rusk, advocated for the unification of all of Korea. They argued that this would represent a huge setback to communism in Asia and would perhaps cause China to question its dependence on Moscow. In fact, these hawks failed to see that the new U.S. naval presence protecting Taiwan and the military assistance to France in Vietnam were probably bringing China and the Soviet Union closer together. Similarly, the joint chiefs, formerly uninterested in Korea, now advocated that MacArthur be allowed to cross the 38th parallel to destroy the North Korean forces, which would otherwise be a recurrent threat.

There were only two voices for a more prudent approach within the government. The State Department's Policy Planning Staff argued that the United States should expel the North Koreans from the south but not cross the 38th parallel to avoid the danger of Soviet or Chinese military intervention. This outlook reflected the influence of its director, George Kennan, one of the premier realist thinkers of the twentieth century, who was in the process of leaving government and whose influence had declined once Acheson replaced Marshall as secretary of state. In the summer of 1950, Kennan prophetically wrote, "The further we were to advance up the peninsula the more unsound it would become from a military standpoint. If we were actually to advance beyond the neck of the peninsula, we would be getting into an area where mass could be used against us and where we would be distinctly at a disadvantage."[15] In addition, the CIA, for its part, warned that crossing the parallel would entail "grave risks" of Chinese military intervention and unspecified Soviet responses.

Nonetheless, as MacArthur built up his forces around Pusan and the Soviets showed no signs of other international military adventures, the tenor of U.S. government discussions moved toward allowing MacArthur to cross the 38th parallel to unite the country. Even U.S. allies seemed to be on board, though London and Paris were always more cautious. On September 9 the National Security Council sent to the president its 81/1 study of U.S. policy regarding crossing the 38th parallel. The document, which Truman signed, anticipated that MacArthur would cross the parallel to destroy the North Korean forces on the condition that there were no signs of major Soviet or Chinese military intervention. Significantly, however, a preliminary draft read, "UN operations should not be permitted to extend into areas close to the Manchurian and USSR borders of Korea." The final draft was amended to read, "U.S. operations should not be permitted to extend across the Manchurian or USSR borders of Korea." The hawks, mainly in the Defense Department and supportive of MacArthur, had managed to push the envelope to allow for operations near the borders.[16]

On September 15 the nature of the debate and the war changed dramatically when MacArthur conducted his bold landing at Inchon, the port of Seoul, despite reservations of the joint chiefs of staff. The risky move, which Mao had warned Kim about to no effect, isolated communist forces in the south. Within two weeks U.S. forces had liberated most of South Korea, though some twenty-five thousand North Korean soldiers managed to straggle back to North Korea. With euphoria in Washington, Truman now authorized MacArthur on September 27 to cross the 38th parallel and destroy the North Korean army, though again with the caveat that he should halt his advance should there be any sign of major Chinese or Soviet intervention. Averell Harriman, a senior Truman adviser, recalled later that it would have taken "a superhuman effort to say no [to crossing the parallel] and to reunification."[17]

South Korean forces crossed the parallel on October 1. Two days later, Chou En-lai, the Chinese foreign minister, told K. M. Panikkar, the Indian ambassador to China, that China would attack U.S.

forces if they also crossed the parallel. Truman, Acheson, and the U.S. military, in their overconfidence, dismissed the warning as bluff and Panikkar as a communist sympathizer. American forces crossed the parallel on October 9.

On October 15 Truman asked MacArthur about the possibility of Chinese intervention at their meeting on Wake Island; the general grandly assured the president that this was highly unlikely, though the Chinese forces would be slaughtered if they did. The fact that Truman asked MacArthur about China's intentions, information that was the province of the CIA, reflected the starry-eyed atmosphere that had surrounded the general since the Inchon success. To be fair to Truman, however, even the CIA now succumbed to wishful thinking and downplayed the likelihood of Chinese intervention. On October 19, the high point of these brief, halcyon autumnal days, U.S. forces captured Pyongyang; photographers took pictures of U.S. officers sitting at Kim's desk.[18]

The euphoria did not last. On October 4 the Chinese politburo decided in favor of Mao's urging for a full-fledged intervention, despite most members' initial opposition. It was not an easy decision, but Beijing did not want a hostile country's forces on its borders. Thus, beginning on October 14, several hundred thousand Chinese soldiers crossed the Yalu River. From October 25 to November 6, Chinese detachments inflicted casualties on South Korean forces and on one U.S. infantry regiment marching toward the Yalu. China's goal in these initial clashes was not to achieve outright military victory but to gain information about South Korean and American forces and to lure them further away from their supply bases to the south before launching a full attack. It was a subtle but effective move requiring considerable self-discipline as the enemy drew even closer to the Chinese border.

Instead of hunkering down in defensible positions at these first signs of Chinese intervention, the international coalition led by the United States paused a single day before continuing north toward the border.[19] No one in Washington felt strong enough to rein in MacArthur and pay the price in Congress. U.S. officials hoped that the new Chinese presence in North Korea, whose size they underestimated, was meant only to deter the American advance. MacArthur promised that U.S. soldiers would be home by Christmas.

MacArthur was right, but those who returned arrived in pine boxes; hundreds of thousands of Chinese soldiers slammed into U.S.-led forces on the night of November 26 to 27. This began one of the longest retreats in American military history; within several weeks, Chinese and North Korean forces had taken Seoul. The joint chiefs and MacArthur swung from overconfidence to excessive fear; the chiefs authorized the field commander to begin planning for the end of the entire Korean commitment and to prepare for a Soviet military attack elsewhere. Acheson called Kennan, who had warned against crossing the 38th parallel, back from his retirement at Princeton University; he read Kennan's eloquent memo to his entire staff as a call for calm determination:

> Dear Mr. Secretary: In international, as in private life, what counts most is not really what happens to someone but how he bears what happens to him. For this reason, almost everything depends on the manner in which we Americans bear what is unquestionably a major failure and disaster to our national fortunes. If we accept it with candor, with dignity, with a resolve to absorb its lessons and to make it good by re-doubled and determined effort—starting all over again, if necessary, along the pattern of Pearl Harbor—we need lose neither our self-confidence nor our allies nor our power for bargaining, eventually, with the Russians. But if we try to conceal from our own people, or from our allies, the full measure of our misfortune, or permit ourselves to seek relief in any reactions of bluster or petulance or hysteria, we can easily find this crisis resolving itself into an irreparable deterioration of our world position—and of our confidence in ourselves.[20]

Could this disaster have been averted through greater American restraint? According to Chinese and Russian archives, the Chinese would not have intervened if the U.S. and South Korean forces had stopped at the 38th parallel, as Kennan and the Policy Planning Staff had advised during the summer. However, there was an even more interesting option. Truman could have ordered MacArthur to cross the parallel and proceed about one hundred miles northward to the narrowest part of North Korea, the so-called neck, and dig in along a hundred-mile line from the capital, Pyongyang, to the port of Wonsan on the east coast. This would have been a defensible line that would have included 90 percent of the entire Korean population. Henry Kissinger advocated this option in this book, *Diplomacy*, though he had the benefit of hindsight. Truman and Acheson did not mention this option in their memoirs.[21]

How would China have reacted to the option of the narrow neck? Chinese archives indicate that Beijing hoped that by intervening in northern North Korea it would deter the Americans from going further than the neck. Beijing planned to occupy the northern part of North Korea, build up its forces over six months, and then decide on next steps. If the Chinese had attacked the Americans at the neck, U.S. air power and artillery would have taken a terrible toll along a defensible line, as they would do during the war starting in the first half of 1951. In any case, stopping at the neck would have left North Korea as a rump state but still a buffer for China.[22]

Granted, it might have been extremely difficult for Washington to force the South Koreans under their headstrong president, Syngman Rhee, to stop at the neck also. If the South Koreans had proceeded on their own toward the Yalu River, China presumably would have intervened. But if the South Koreans had had any sense they would have retreated quickly to the neck as soon as Chinese intervention seemed imminent. As it was, they retreated quickly when the Chinese intervened in late November, leaving the tougher fighting to the Americans and other Western forces. Granted, MacArthur would have been furious at the order to stop at the neck after taking Pyongyang on October 19 and would have taken his case to Republican hawks in Congress. However, President Truman could have told him to follow orders or to resign.

In any case, the Chinese intervention was a disaster, but not a debacle. The Marines in particular retreated in an orderly fashion and did not abandon their wounded or even their frozen dead. Part of their success was due to the prudent decision of commander Major General Oliver Smith to ignore MacArthur's reckless orders to proceed northward during September and October without taking the usual precautions about maintaining adequate supply lines. The Americans and other UN forces carried out a generally well-organized retreat; their heroism was exemplary.

Now, it was time for Chinese hubris. On December 4, Mao ordered the Chinese commander in Korea, Peng Dehuai, to cross the 38th parallel, take Seoul, destroy the South Korean army, and continue southward to force all U.S. forces to withdraw from Korea. Peng answered that he would follow orders but that the Americans were fighting well.[23]

General Matthew Ridgway, who took over the command of army forces in December, stabilized the front roughly fifty miles south of Seoul in part by purging less competent offices. After blunting a massive Chinese offensive on New Year's Eve, U.S.-led forces pushed northward under Ridgway's command in January and February. At times, they inflicted ten times as many casualties on the Chinese as they suffered, thanks to their superior artillery and aerial support. By April, Ridgway had pushed 25 to 40 miles north of the parallel to a better defensive line.[24]

MacArthur, still based in Japan, argued publicly that US/UN forces should take the aerial and naval war to China to unify all of Korea; and he reached out to conservative Republicans in Congress to make his case. But as he had less credibility in Washington after the November disaster, Truman relieved him of his command in April 1951 for refusing to agree to the new Washington strategy of limiting U.S. ground forces to south of the 38th parallel and not attacking targets in China itself. MacArthur was lionized by Republicans and much of the public, but after the joint chiefs explained their reasons for supporting Truman's move, public acclaim began to fade.[25]

With the war beginning to turn against them, the Chinese communists proposed negotiations to end the war in June 1951. Having been scalded by the Chinese intervention, the United States became too risk-averse and let up on its aerial and naval attacks against targets in North Korea. This allowed the Chinese to take advantage of their talent for fortifications and camouflage. Since they had little to gain at the negotiating table (US-led forces had not occupied large chunks of North Korea with which to bargain), they settled in for a protracted war. As a result, more Americans were killed during two years of negotiations than during the first year of the war. Finally, some combination of the Soviets and the Chinese tiring of the stalemate, President Eisenhower's warnings about the use of nuclear weapons, and Stalin's death brought the war to an end in the summer of 1953.[26]

Despite Truman's great achievement in defending South Korea, his administration violated several fundamental tenets of effective statecraft. Truman and Acheson acted imprudently by not matching means to ends. While they were more committed to South Korea's independence than Congress and the Defense Department, they withdrew U.S. combat forces from South Korea in the summer of 1949, leaving only a modest training component. This represented an ineffective middle path between a total withdrawal and a full, serious commitment.

Moreover, Truman's and Acheson's commitment to South Korea was undermined by the Defense Department's emphasis on worst-case-scenario thinking. Because the Defense Department was too wary of a frontal Soviet attack on Europe, it slighted planning to counter the much more likely Soviet actions along other parts of the Soviet periphery. Stalin, though relentless in probing for Western weakness, was not reckless; he preferred stealth and indirection to frontal assaults. Ironically, a certain imprudence led the United States to focus excessively on the worst-case scenario in Europe to the detriment of Asia.

Another failure to exercise prudence was the leadership's unwillingness to rein in General MacArthur's military dash toward the Chinese border following his victory at Inchon. Aware of the risk of Chinese intervention, the military ordered MacArthur to send only South Korean forces to the Chinese border but acquiesced when he ignored the directive. Dean Acheson's memoirs refer to Washington's increased unease after the Chinese first intervened for several weeks in late October in the northern reaches of North Korea. Yet no one was willing to go to Truman with these growing concerns despite the fact that the option of withdrawing to the narrow neck between Pyongyang and Wonsan, as Kennan advised from outside the government, was there for the taking. Instead, Truman and his advisers made the perfect the enemy of the (very) good: they fell victim to groupthink, the tendency of decision-makers and advisers to coalesce around a policy for the sake of group solidarity.[27]

This imprudence overlapped with the difficulties that Truman and his advisers faced in understanding the admittedly complex and fluid situation facing them in the Korean peninsula. They never understood that once the Chinese Communist Party took power in

1949, China could turn its intentions to uniting the two Koreas under communist rule. Such a victory would also free up North Korean forces fighting in China. If U.S. leaders had anticipated the full impact of the impending communist victory in China, they might not have withdrawn combat forces from South Korea in the summer of 1949.[28]

Moreover, Truman and his advisers failed to grasp the implications of the conditions on the fast-changing battlefield. After succumbing to hubris after the Inchon breakthrough, they became too risk-averse after the Chinese intervention. They did not realize that U.S. forces had succeeded in turning the tide of war in the spring of 1951, thereby bringing the Chinese communists to the bargaining table that summer. Instead, they reduced air and artillery operations, the United States' strong suit, as a sign of goodwill and in hopes of reducing the incentives for the Chinese to send more troops to the battlefront. In doing so, the caricature of numberless Asian hordes replaced the earlier image of second-rate Asian conscripts. The president and his advisers did not understand that diplomacy and war are not always distinct activities, but sometimes complementary ones. Maintaining greater military pressure probably would have ended the war earlier. As Frederick the Great reportedly remarked, diplomacy without arms is like an orchestra without instruments.[29]

Historians have often focused on the dramatic and willful MacArthur, with his brilliant breakthrough at Inchon and the subsequent Chinese intervention, in apportioning blame for the Korea disaster. However, Truman and his senior advisers, who were neither willful nor impulsive, made the key mistakes. Before the war broke out, they were too dovish insofar as they withdrew combat forces. During the first year of the war they were too hawkish in acquiescing to MacArthur's march toward the Chinese border. During the last two years of negotiations they eased up on military pressure in an overreaction to Chinese intervention. None of this detracts from their major achievement of saving South Korea, but the costs could have been much less lower or avoided altogether if they had better understood the complexity of the situation and exercised greater prudence. As Acheson said, "I have an unhappy conviction, that none of us, myself prominently included, served him [Truman] as he was entitled to be served."[30]

CHAPTER 7

Nixon and Kissinger in the 1973 Arab-Israeli War

The Ability to Adapt and Anticipate, and the Mastery of Complex Negotiations

Like Truman and Acheson in Korea, President Richard Nixon and Secretary of State Henry Kissinger were caught by surprise by the outbreak of the 1973 Arab-Israeli War. But unlike Truman and Acheson after the success at Inchon and the Chinese intervention, they did not overreact to the battlefield conditions on the ground. They knew what they wanted to accomplish from the outset of hostilities: a rough military stalemate followed by negotiations that would reduce the likelihood of renewed hostilities. During the twenty-day war and subsequent negotiations, Kissinger was in charge of the day-to-day implementation of policy but Nixon provided the overall policy guidance. Increasingly, however, the president withdrew from daily policy-making as the Watergate scandal closed in.

The president and his secretary of state nearly always agreed about policy goals and implementation. Initially they favored a low-profile approach, assuming, like many observers, that the Israelis would win quickly, as they had done in 1967. Then, when it became clear that this war would be longer and more difficult, Nixon and Kissinger supported Israel with a military airlift to help it to regain its military footing and to force Egypt and Syria to agree to a cease-fire.

Finally, Nixon and Kissinger backed Egypt to prevent a one-sided Israeli victory toward the end of the war.

Nixon's and Kissinger's policies illustrate several important and recurrent foreign policy principles. Their successful combination of steadfast strategic goals with tactical flexibility in the face of changing circumstances recalls the approach of George Washington, who abandoned his initial conventional approach to pursue a hybrid guerrilla-war strategy before returning to conventional warfare at Yorktown. Similarly, their flexibility about whether to focus on helping Israel or Egypt in light of changing military circumstances resembles Washington's and Hamilton's ability to navigate between Britain and France from the 1770s to the 1790s. Moreover, Nixon's and Kissinger's goal of a rough balance of power between Israel and Egypt, with no single decisive victor or vanquished, resembled Theodore Roosevelt's mediation efforts between Russia and Japan. Finally, Kissinger's use of guile during nearly two years of negotiations after the war resembled Franklin Roosevelt's policy before World War II. Yet Kissinger, like Theodore Roosevelt, was generally frank with the parties, explaining to each the domestic situation of the other and recommending specific ideas about compromises.

The Arab attack on Israel on October 6, 1973, caught nearly the entire world by surprise, including the U.S. and Israeli governments. Both countries had erroneously assumed that the Arabs would not launch a war that they were likely to lose, and U.S. leaders assumed that if Israel was not worried about an attack, then there was no reason for them to be concerned. Israel, for its part, thought that the soonest the Arabs might attack would be later in the 1970s, if and when they received long-range missiles from Moscow that could target Israeli cities—a reasonable assumption but one that turned out to be wrong. Moreover, the wily Kissinger had been conducting secret talks, at Nixon's behest, with the Israelis and the Egyptians at the United Nations and (unbeknownst to the U.S. State Department) planned to begin substantive negotiations after the October 1973 Israeli national elections. So, Kissinger reasoned, why would Egypt go to war if there was a diplomatic option? Yet Egypt felt, understandably, that it would not get much from Israel at the bargaining table without demonstrating that the Arabs had a serious military option.[1]

Unlike leaders in Washington and Jerusalem, Egyptian president Sadat understood that Clausewitz's dictum that war is politics by other means applied to the situation at hand. Sadat and Syrian president Hafez al-Assad planned to launch a war not to defeat the Israelis militarily but to inflict enough damage to force them to make major concessions at the negotiating table. They also thought—correctly, as it turned out—that not just the Soviets but perhaps even the Americans would prevent a complete Israeli victory.

Interestingly, Nixon was one of the few U.S. government officials who thought in early 1973 that war was likely that year and that the Arabs would use the oil weapon. He had no special information, but rather a well-honed understanding of international affairs based on years of senior-level experience, and a brooding tendency to think that if things could go wrong in life they probably would. This did not make him risk-averse; rather, he was grimly determined to soldier on through adversity, albeit in a somewhat fatalistic manner.[2]

When the war broke out on October 6, the entire U.S. government mistakenly assumed that the Israelis would win a quick victory, as they had in 1967. The United States would therefore pursue a prudent low-profile approach. It would not criticize the Arabs for their attack and would send only modest amounts of arms to Israel. Larger amounts would be unnecessary and would anger the Arabs and perhaps provoke the Soviets into countermoves. William Quandt, then a senior National Security Council official for the Middle East, recounts that Kissinger told senior U.S. government colleagues on the first day of the war that Washington would try to work with the Soviet Union to reestablish a cease-fire on the basis of the status-quo ante. According to an overly confident Kissinger, the Arabs in their "demented state" would oppose that position, but would embrace it once the Israeli counteroffensive gained traction. Thus, a U.S. position that initially appeared to be pro-Israeli would soon seem pro-Arab.[3]

On October 7 and 8 the CIA estimated that the Israelis would win the war conclusively within a week. Kissinger did not dispute this but was puzzled that the Arabs were not calling for a cease-fire if they were about to lose. For his part, Nixon accurately forecast the evolution of the war: "They'll cut the Egyptians off. Poor dumb Egyptians, getting across the Canal and all the bridges will be blown up.... Go over and destroy the SAM [surface-to-air] missile sites."

He also expressed his greatest concern to Kissinger, which was not the war itself but the Israeli intransigence likely if they won a decisive victory: "The one thing we have to be concerned about . . . is that the Israelis, when they finish clobbering the Egyptians and the Syrians, which they will do, will be even more impossible to deal with than before, and you and I have got to determine in our minds, we must have a diplomatic settlement here. . . . We must not tell them that now, but we have got to do it. You see, they could feel so strong as a result of this, they'd say: Well, why do we have to settle?"[4]

Nixon's ambivalence toward the Israeli position at the beginning of the war reflected his overall views on the diplomatic impasse. During his first years in office, Nixon told Kissinger in private that they, perhaps in conjunction with the Soviet Union, should aggressively pressure Israel to return Arab territory. Nixon would never follow up, however, probably because he was dubious of his ability to force major Israeli concessions. He had also seen firsthand the unsuccessful Eisenhower policy of forcing Israel to withdraw from the entire Sinai in 1957, allowing Nasser to claim victory to his uncomprehending population and thereby making him more aggressive, not less.

On October 9, however, Israeli ambassador Simcha Dinitz woke Kissinger at 1:45 a.m. to tell him that the war had become much more difficult than the Israelis had anticipated, and that they needed large amounts of U.S. arms. Egypt and Syria, with new Soviet anti-tank and antiaircraft missiles, had punched five to ten miles beyond the 1967 cease-fire lines and were causing serious damage, particularly to Israeli tanks in the Sinai and Israeli aircraft over the Golan Heights on the Syrian front. At least fifty thousand Egyptians had crossed the Suez Canal under the cover of surface-to-air missiles, and the Syrians were fighting cohesively, even if in retreat. As one Israeli general dryly commented about the Arabs, when you play chess with someone who is good at chess, you get better at chess. Nixon and Kissinger agreed to send munitions immediately and heavier weapons later if necessary. Other advisers, such as Defense Secretary James Schlesinger, were skeptical that Israel really was in trouble and wondered if they were not exaggerating their dire situation.[5]

On October 10 the Soviets stepped up their resupply airlift, particularly for the deteriorating Syrian front, where the Israelis had gone beyond the 1967 cease-fire line despite tough resistance. Nixon,

Kissinger, and Schlesinger began a modest military supply effort to Israel but still wanted to keep a low profile. They therefore sought to charter civilian transport for the air supply rather than use U.S. Defense Department aircraft. When the charter idea proved impractical, they transported arms to the Portuguese Azores for pickup by the Israelis instead of flying them directly to Tel Aviv.

At this point, Kissinger wanted the Israelis to regain their initial prewar military position or perhaps advance modestly beyond it to disabuse the Arabs of the notion that they had serious military options with Soviet arms. Kissinger also told colleagues that it would be important for Washington to be seen as a reliable partner by Jerusalem during the war to make it more amenable to concessions afterward. Nonetheless, Quandt believes that Kissinger and perhaps Nixon and the Defense Department held back to some degree on the airlift supply to pressure the Israeli government into accepting a cease-fire.[6]

On October 12 the Israelis told Kissinger that they would agree to a cease-fire in principle, presumably because of their high rate of casualties. Israeli intelligence also told Prime Minister Golda Meir that Sadat was not interested in a cease-fire yet, so Israel could make a gesture of being reasonable without having to follow through. Sadat, for his part, wanted to reach the Mitla and Giddi passes, about twenty miles or about one-fifth into the entire Sinai, to relieve Israeli pressure on the Syrian front, improve his bargaining position for the postwar negotiations, and score a concrete military achievement for his public.

The refusal of a cease-fire by Sadat and Assad ushered in the second phase of U.S. policy, in which Washington sided with Israel by launching a major airlift. Nixon and Kissinger sought not a decisive Israeli victory, but rather an end to the fighting as quickly as possible. This would require more Israeli military progress to convince the Arabs to agree to a cease-fire. Moreover, under no circumstances did Nixon and Kissinger want the United States to be outdone by the growing Soviet airlift. Nixon also may have been responding to pro-Israeli congressional pressure just as the Watergate scandal was worsening.[7]

On October 14 giant U.S. military C-5 transport planes landed for the first time in Tel Aviv's Lod Airport with military supplies. Kissinger told the Soviets and the Arab countries that the airlift would stop if the Soviets stopped theirs. The same day, however, Israel turned the military tide without the direct benefit of the new U.S. supplies by pummeling Egyptian forces leaving the cover of their surface-to-air missile defenses in an unsuccessful attempt to reach the Mitla and Giddi passes. This victory enabled the Israelis to launch a counteroffensive on the night of October 15–16 in which their forces crossed the canal and turned south to cut off the Egyptian Third Army from its supply lines from Cairo.[8]

With the new military situation, Nixon and Kissinger turned toward fostering negotiations between the parties. On October 17 Nixon told four Arab foreign ministers at the White House that he could not promise a full Israeli withdrawal to the 1967 borders, but that he would make a good-faith effort at serious negotiations. That same day, Arab oil ministers announced they would cut oil production by 5 percent each month until Israel had withdrawn from all Arab territories. The oil embargo, which lasted until March 1974, would be an irritating but manageable factor in the coming diplomacy.

On October 21 Kissinger flew to Moscow to negotiate a cease-fire. The Soviets initially proposed linking it to deep Israeli withdrawals, but they dropped this idea for a simple cease-fire in place. The Israelis, now in a superior military position, reluctantly agreed to the cease-fire proposal just as a decisive victory was within their grasp. The guns fell silent on October 22, but not for long. Israeli forces continued to push forward here and there until they had surrounded the Third Army, thereby cutting it off from water and food supplies from Cairo.

Kissinger stopped in Israel on his return from Moscow to Washington to sell the cease-fire proposal to Israeli leaders, though Middle East scholar and former U.S. diplomat Martin Indyk believes that he may not have argued forcefully enough about the importance of adhering to an agreement.[9] In any case, on October 24 a desperate Sadat called publicly on the United States and the Soviet Union to send military forces to prevent the Third Army from having to surrender. U.S. intelligence noted the increased alert status of airborne divisions in the Soviet Union, the presence of amphibious landing craft with the Soviet fleet in the eastern Mediterranean, and indications of nuclear cargo on Soviet ships heading toward the Egyptian port of Alexandria.

In fact, the situation was even more tense than this worrisome intelligence indicated. Nixon was seeking solace in alcohol from the growing Watergate scandal, and a sleep-deprived Leonid Brezhnev was beside himself at the prospect of another Arab rout. Brezhnev sent a personal message to Nixon late in the night of October 24 to 25, warning that Moscow planned to intervene militarily either jointly with the United States or unilaterally, if necessary, to end the fighting.

Nixon and Kissinger strongly opposed the reintroduction of Soviet military forces in Egypt. With Nixon's approval, Kissinger authorized the heightened alert of U.S. military forces, including nuclear aircraft, as a signal to Moscow to stand back, and the Defense Department began preparing contingency plans for sending U.S. military forces to the region. Kissinger also sent a back-channel message to Sadat in Nixon's name saying that Kissinger would not visit Cairo to start negotiations if the Soviets intervened. Both the Soviets and Sadat backed away from the idea of military intervention, but the Egyptian president continued to implore Nixon to force the Israelis to permit the resupply of the Third Army. It remains unclear whether the Soviets genuinely intended to deploy military forces in the Sinai to save the Third Army or simply to send a threatening signal to Israel. Neither Israel nor the United States wanted to find out.[10]

At this point, Nixon and Kissinger began the third and final stage of U.S. policy during the war, saving the beleaguered Egyptian Third Army and, with it, the prospects for serious negotiations. As mentioned, their goal from the start of the war was to use the anticipated Israeli victory as a springboard for serious negotiations, including Israeli withdrawals from territories captured in the 1967 war. To this end, Kissinger applied his considerable psychological acuity to understanding the parties' psyches. He felt the Arabs had to restore their sense of dignity through a respectable performance on the battlefield; this would help their leaders make necessary concessions before their own domestic audiences. He also understood the Israeli psyche but did not allow it to deter him from his diplomatic goals: "Maddened by the fact that they had been surprised, beside themselves with grief over the high casualties, deeply distrustful of Sadat . . . Israeli leaders wanted to end the war with his destruction. Their emotion was understandable. But one of our interests was to give Arab leaders an incentive for moderation. Our [diplomatic] exchanges with Cairo [going back to 1972] had convinced us that Anwar Sadat represented the best chance for moderate peace in the Middle East."[11]

Senior U.S. officials were now ready to lean heavily on the Israelis. By October 26 Defense Secretary Schlesinger was proposing to resupply the Egyptian Third Army with U.S. C-130 aircraft and to cut off the U.S. airlift to Israel to pressure them to release their stranglehold over the Third Army. Nixon, though preoccupied by Watergate, seemed open to these options.

Kissinger was uneasy about an abrupt end to the airlift and felt it might tempt Arab intransigence and result in renewed Soviet intervention. At the same time, he did not spare the Israelis in blunt exchanges with Ambassador Dinitz: "He [Nixon] wanted to make it absolutely clear that we cannot permit the destruction of the Egyptian army. . . . It is an option that does not exist. . . . [We require] an [Israeli] answer that permits some sort of negotiation and some sort of positive response on the nonmilitary supplies, or we will join the other members of the Security Council in making it an international matter. I have to say again, your course is suicidal. You will not be permitted to destroy this army. You are destroying the possibility for negotiations."[12]

On October 27 Kissinger told Dinitz, "If you could, for once, be positive quickly. I have requests to stop the [U.S.] airlift [to Israel], to have U.S. forces do the supplying [to Egypt]. Our government is going crazy."[13]

On October 28 Israeli and Egyptian military officers met for direct talks for the first time since the 1949 armistice talks, and the first Egyptian convoy with food, water, and medicine arrived the next day. The Third Army would not be forced to surrender; the turn away from war and toward negotiations had begun.

Postwar Negotiations: From a Tenuous Cease-Fire to Stability and Peace

With a tenuous cease-fire in place, Kissinger embarked on negotiations that would end up taking almost two years to help usher in peace between Israel and Egypt and an uneasy stability between Israel and Syria on the Golan Heights. However, in the immediate aftermath of the war, progress seemed doubtful. The Israeli and Egyptian armies were entangled with one another, and the Israeli army had pushed the Syrian army back to about twenty miles from Damascus. At the outset of the negotiations, the Egyptian and Syrian governments wanted Israel to return to the 1967 borders and cede the West Bank to the Palestine Liberation Organization. Nor was it clear what Cairo and Damascus would be willing to offer in return for their optimal demands. Jerusalem, for its part, was deeply mistrustful of the Arab parties; Syria would not even tell Israel which prisoners of war it held.

Faced with these seemingly irreconcilable positions, Kissinger sought to disaggregate the issues that separated the parties. He had never liked previous ambitious diplomatic mediation attempts, notably by UN mediator Gunnar Jarring and U.S. Secretary of State William Rogers, to solve all the major issues in one grand bargain. In contrast, Kissinger sought a series of partial or step-by-step agreements that would be difficult to achieve, but not impossible. These partial agreements could defuse the immediate dangers of renewed combat and perhaps build trust over time among the parties. This in turn could enable the parties to tackle increasingly difficult issues. Proceeding in a piecemeal manner was Kissinger's overarching strategic approach to the conflict.

Kissinger began his search for an initial Israeli-Egyptian agreement when he met President Sadat for the first time in Cairo on November 7. The Egyptian president wanted an immediate Israeli retreat to the October 22 cease-fire lines to relieve pressure on his surrounded Third Army. Sadat's foreign minister in Washington had already told Kissinger that Egypt would then want Israel to withdraw two-thirds of the way across the Sinai to the El-Arish–Ras Muhammad line in return for some modest concessions.

Kissinger was concerned that the October 22 line would be difficult to relocate and, even if agreed upon, would not guarantee an end to the fighting. He knew from his talks with the Israeli cabinet that a major withdrawal into the Sinai would not be possible as part of an initial agreement. Kissinger therefore suggested to Sadat that they try for something more than the October 22 lines—getting Israeli troops off the canal's west bank entirely—but not too ambitious. Such a withdrawal would take more time than a return to the vague October 22 lines, he explained, but it would involve an equal amount of diplomatic capital with a bigger payoff for Egypt. In the meantime, Egypt, with U.S. help, could seek an immediate agreement with Israel to relieve pressure on the Third Army. Kissinger underlined that he would pursue whatever option Sadat wanted, though he thought the immediate agreement to be followed by an Israeli evacuation from the canal's west bank would be best. Sadat hesitated and then agreed to Kissinger's proposal. As Kissinger explained in his memoirs, "It was the contemplation of these alternative risks—of bogging down in niggling detail and of consuming our energies in the pursuit of comprehensive goals that induced us to decide instead on a step-by-step approach."[14]

Within several days in November, Kissinger negotiated the first Egyptian-Israeli agreement whereby Cairo released its Israeli prisoners of war (as Israel did with its Egyptian prisoners) in return for a UN presence along the supply road from Cairo, thereby ensuring the transport of food, supplies, and medicine by Egyptian trucks.

Kissinger's approach to this first agreement established a pattern. He first persuaded Sadat to defer excessively difficult goals (deep Israeli withdrawals into the Sinai) in favor of an easier concession (removal of Israeli forces from the canal's west bank), but not the absolute easiest option (return to the October 22 lines). Once he had persuaded Sadat to pursue the middle option, Kissinger sought an immediate agreement in which he focused on the core issues: prisoner exchange, the Israeli priority, and supply modalities, the Egyptian priority. A final issue, an Israeli demand that Egypt promise not to blockade ships at the Strait of Bab el-Mandeb, leading to the Israeli port of Eilat, then fell into place because Egypt had refrained from doing so during the war. This pattern, in which Kissinger carved out achievable objectives and a manageable cluster of issues but then focused on the most important and difficult issues within that cluster, would be repeated in subsequent negotiations.

With the front lines along the canal stabilized and an Israeli election having taken place in December, Kissinger turned to negotiate a more ambitious agreement between Israel and Egypt. Defense Minister Moshe Dayan came to Washington on January 4, 1974, to present Israel's opening position. Israel proposed withdrawing its troops from the canal's west bank to the west side of the Mitla and Giddi passes, twenty to thirty miles into the Sinai, but it wanted few Egyptian soldiers and no tanks or artillery to remain on the east bank of the canal. Dayan also presented several political conditions, notably the opening of the canal, which had been closed since the 1967 war, the rebuilding of the cities along it, and a public declaration ending the state of belligerency.

Kissinger then embarked on five days of shuttle diplomacy between Jerusalem and Cairo. He was generally straightforward with the parties, telling them what he thought the other party would and would not accept. When, for example, Sadat asked his advice about the Israeli position, Kissinger said he thought that the Israelis would not withdraw behind the passes as part of an initial agreement but that they might make concessions on the disarmament zones.

At the same time, he engaged periodically in subtle forms of manipulation to nudge the parties in the right direction. When, for example, he conveyed the initial Israeli position to Sadat on January 12, he omitted the broader Israeli political demands. He reasoned that if the negotiations about disengagement proved difficult, these political demands would make matters worse; if there was progress on disengagement, the political demands could be handled more easily. He mentioned the political demands therefore on his next trip back to Cairo once the negotiations had gained some momentum. Similarly, Kissinger initially withheld an Israeli concession about the amount of Egyptian artillery on the east bank to offer it to Sadat later in return for Egyptian concessions on the locations of surface-to-air missile defense systems, an Israeli priority. To the Israeli cabinet, he exaggerated how hard he had bargained with Sadat for positions favorable for Israel, which was sometimes, but not always, the case. On several occasions he offered an "American proposal" that the parties could accept that they would not have accepted from each other. While he engaged in tactical guile in the timing of concessions, generally he was quite straightforward in communicating to each party what he thought the other was willing to offer and to accept.

Before Kissinger's last trip to Jerusalem during the January 1974 shuttle, Sadat told Kissinger that as a sign of goodwill, he would not exercise his right, according to the agreement, to station thirty tanks across the canal. He asked the U.S. secretary to take a personal message to Prime Minister Meir: "You must take my word seriously. When I made my [diplomatic] initiative in 1971, I meant it. When

I threatened war, I meant it. When I talk of peace now, I mean it."[15] It was the first message ever from an Egyptian political leader to an Israeli counterpart. The two sides reached the disengagement agreement on January 17, 1974.[16]

The January 1974 accord, like the November 1973 agreement, helped to reduce the level of distrust on both sides and established precedents for future Israeli withdrawals toward the 1967 border in return for Egyptian force-limitation zones in the evacuated territory and political gestures. As was the case with the November 1973 agreement, once the parties had agreed not to seek a comprehensive solution to all the issues separating them, they concentrated on the most important and usually most difficult sticking points. Once Sadat had agreed to only a modest Israeli withdrawal to the western side of the Sinai passes, the parties first negotiated the location of the new Israeli forward line, then the composition of the limited-force zones, and finally the less pressing Israeli political demands. Thus, Kissinger pursued a partial approach on the strategic level by deferring the most difficult issues, the entire Sinai evacuation and diplomatic recognition. Once a potential agreement began to emerge, he confronted the most difficult issues head-on, despite sometimes craftily withholding temporarily positions of the parties to facilitate the negotiations.

The May 1974 Syrian-Israeli agreement proved to be much more difficult. Whereas the sparsely inhabited Sinai acted as a natural buffer, the Golan Heights was a much smaller area. Moreover, whereas Sadat was willing to forgo marginal negotiating gains to foster a positive atmosphere for subsequent negotiations, Assad and the Israelis bargained over every kilometer, every hill. Israel did want an agreement, however, to obtain the return of its POWs and to end the ongoing trickle of casualties. Syria wanted the return of the territory it had lost in the 1973 fighting, thereby pushing the Israelis back from the Damascus area, in addition to the small town of Qunaitra, capital of the Golan Heights, which it had lost in the 1967 war. This would allow Assad to show his people that the 1973 war had not been in vain. Kissinger wanted an agreement to stabilize the Golan front, reduce Sadat's isolation in the Arab world to allow him to proceed with another deal with Israel, and encourage the lifting of the Saudis' oil embargo.

Kissinger therefore shuttled back and forth between Jerusalem and Damascus as both sides negotiated tenaciously over the line of Israeli withdrawal and the status of Qunaitra. As in the Egyptian negotiations, Kissinger demonstrated several attributes of a successful negotiator. First, he displayed a remarkable stamina that allowed him to negotiate deep into the night and at times to wear down his interlocutors. Second, he quickly sized up the key issues and focused on the most important one, the line of Israeli withdrawal. He assumed correctly that other issues would fall into place once this line of separation was agreed upon, notably the role of the UN forces, the modalities of the limited-force zones, the POWs, and measures concerning Palestinian terrorists operating from Syrian territory. Third, he used all his guile to push the parties forward by doling out their respective compromises at the optimal time and by mastering the military arcana about the limited-force zones. Fourth, while Kissinger blamed the Israelis for dragging out the negotiations and, reportedly, for turning him into a rug merchant hawking his wares between both capitals, he never personalized these disagreements. Thanks to his efforts, Israel and Syria finally reached an agreement after thirty days of intense negotiations.

The agreement held. While Israel and Syria would fight each other in Lebanon in the air and on the ground in the early 1980s and the Israeli air force would strike Iranian targets in Syria in the twenty-first century, the two sides generally adhered to the agreement that Kissinger brought about. In the Golan Heights there would be decades of relative quiet.[17]

The second Sinai accord of August 1975 proved to be more difficult because the Israelis had no incentive to bring large numbers of their troops back from their exposed and financially costly positions along the Suez Canal. At a minimum, Sadat wanted Israel to withdraw behind the Giddi and Mitla passes and to evacuate the Abu Rudeis oil fields in the southern Sinai, which supplied about half of Israel's oil needs. Israel, now led by a triumvirate of Yitzhak Rabin, Shimon Peres, and Yigal Allon, wanted a declaration of nonbelligerency and favorable terms regarding force-limitation zones from any evacuated territory.

In November and December 1974, Kissinger was able to clarify each side's position during visits to Cairo and Jerusalem. He told the

Israelis that Egypt would not formally end the state of belligerency because of opposition from the rest of the Arab world and that they should concentrate on the functional equivalents of nonbelligerency, such as the end of the economic boycott.

Evacuating the Sinai passes would not be easy for Israel because they had real military value. Twenty miles long, they represented the best way for armies to advance through the otherwise inhospitable terrain. Moreover, Israel had an early warning station at the west side of the passes that provided valuable intelligence about Egyptian military preparations in case of an attack. The Israelis also had a nearby air base that contributed to their forward defense. Finally, the oil fields met about 50 to 60 percent of Israel's oil requirements. All this meant that the Israelis would not give up these assets easily.

In March 1975 Kissinger left for the Middle East in search of a second Sinai agreement. In Cairo, Sadat agreed to consider a formula based on the non-use of force but not a pledge of nonbelligerency. He also agreed to modify the economic boycott but insisted that his army must regain control possession of all of the Sinai passes and oil fields. After Kissinger spent ten days shuttling between the two capitals, Israel agreed to cede the oil fields but not a road connecting them to the Egyptian zone. It still refused to evacuate all of the passes in the absence of a nonbelligerency pledge. Kissinger told the Israelis that this would not be enough for Sadat and returned to Washington.

Kissinger and President Gerald Ford blamed Israel privately for not offering more to Egypt and criticized Israeli leaders more elliptically in congressional briefings. Despite the political risk, they put all-new arms contracts for Israeli military aid on hold. While they had the support of much of the congressional leadership, seventy-six senators signed a letter, at the bidding of the Israeli lobby, urging the administration to be responsive to Israel's defense needs. Presumably, many of them knew they were putting the Israeli government's short-term interests ahead of American and longer-term Israeli interests. Nonetheless, President Ford did not flinch in his willingness to take on the Israeli lobby.

Sadat, for his part, suggested to Ford and Kissinger that American military personnel could supervise the early warning station in the passes if that would reassure the Israelis, and he agreed that

Egypt would extend the mandate of the UN buffer zone between the two sides.

In September 1975 the Israelis finally agreed to remove their forces from the passes in addition to returning the oil fields. Several factors had contributed to their change of heart. Rabin and the cabinet had shown the Israeli public that they had stood up to the Americans, but they now wanted to reopen the American arms-supply channel and to avoid a long-term falling-out with Washington. Sadat's reopening of the Suez Canal also assuaged some Israeli fears about his intentions. Jerusalem was slowly coming around to the idea that Sadat was serious about ending the cycle of wars that had begun in 1948.[18]

Tactical Flexibility and Strategic Steadfastness

Were there any differences between Nixon and Kissinger during this period? Before the war Nixon sometimes mused about trying to impose a Soviet-U.S. agreement on Israel, something Kissinger never took seriously. Nixon himself never pursued the idea during the war when it was a theoretical option. However, Nixon, along with the Defense Department, was more willing to consider applying dramatic pressure, notably suspending arms deliveries to Israel and ordering the U.S. Army to supply the surrounded Egyptians. Kissinger feared these measures might raise unrealistic expectations among the Arabs, draw the Soviet military back in the region, and make Israel even more distrustful during the postwar negotiations. These reasonable policy differences proved to be relatively minor insofar as Kissinger, with Nixon's backing, was able to browbeat the Israeli ambassador and ultimately the Israeli cabinet into releasing the Third Army.

Nixon and Kissinger also felt it best to avoid an ill-defined middle-path policy between Israel and Egypt. Instead, they came down clearly on Israel's side by sending it arms and munitions to encourage Sadat to seek a cease-fire and to check the Soviet airlift. However, once the tide of the war shifted in favor of the Israelis, the United States pressed Israel not to force the Egyptian Third Army to surrender.

During the postwar negotiations, Kissinger displayed tenacity and an understanding of complex political-military situations. He pursued a partial approach by creating clusters of solvable issues rather than seeking a comprehensive settlement. Like Franklin Roosevelt, Kissinger was guileful about his ultimate goals. According to Prime Minister Yitzhak Rabin, "In one of our less heated, private conversations I asked Kissinger to satisfy my curiosity on one point. 'We've known one another for years and have held hundreds of conversations on every subject under the sun. Yet I have never heard you express your view about what Israel's borders ought to be. Now that we're alone, just the two of us.' Smiling back at me, Kissinger said: 'You've never heard it, and you won't hear it now. I hope that when the times comes to decide on Israel's borders. I shall no longer be serving as Secretary of State.'"[19] However, Kissinger would be quite blunt and direct with all the parties during the partial agreement negotiations. After initial discussions, he would put forward his own ideas and focus on the key issues. Thus, he would avoid the most difficult issues on the strategic level and focus on the thorniest ones at the tactical level.

As mentioned, Kissinger succeeded in part because he did not personalize his differences with the parties' leaders, particularly the Israelis. While Woodrow Wilson turned the League of Nations proposal into a kind of winner-take-all contest with his American critics, Kissinger never did this with his foreign counterparts. He could even deal with the main Israeli lobby group, the American Israel Political Action Committee (AIPAC), with humor, even though its actions were probably encouraging Israel to stiffen its position and making the negotiations more difficult for Kissinger. When, for example, Kissinger offered economic assistance to Syrian president Assad as an incentive to reach an agreement in 1974, a senior AIPAC official told Kissinger's deputy that the organization wanted to be helpful, but that it might have to oppose the proposal unless the package included additional assistance to Israel. Kissinger replied the next day through his deputy, "This is the most outrageous idea that I have heard since coming to Washington. It is utterly preposterous. And one more thing: You have yourself a deal."[20]

And so did the Egyptians, Syrians, and Israelis, thanks to the efforts of Nixon and Kissinger.

CHAPTER 8

Carter and Brzezinski and the Fall of the Shah of Iran

Values and Interests

Jimmy Carter was the first president since Woodrow Wilson to dispar-age the role of power in international politics. In fact, Carter's favorite president was Wilson: he wrote, "Like him, I felt I was taking office at a time when Americans desired a return to first principles by their government. His [Wilson's] call for national repentance also seemed ap-propriate." Carter felt that American foreign policy since Truman had been too focused on great power competition with the Soviets and not enough on human rights advocacy: "Much of the time we failed to ex-hibit as an American characteristic the idealism of Jefferson or Wilson."[1]

Like Wilson, Carter had something of a self-righteous, judgmental strain. A straight arrow, Carter grew up in rural Georgia and enjoyed teaching the Bible to Sunday school classes. While the Old Testament contains many stories of statecraft and war, it was the moral homi-lies and pacifism of the New Testament that probably captured his imagination.

President Carter was more comfortable with diplomacy unlinked to military force. His major achievements—and they were substan-tial—were in the realm of this kind of diplomacy, notably the Israel-Egypt peace treaty, the establishment of diplomatic relations with China, and the Panama Canal Treaty. To his credit, these required the expenditure of political capital and sometimes political risk.

However, Carter was less successful with security issues. He was rather passive about Soviet and Cuban military and political advances in Angola, Ethiopia, and Afghanistan. He was also clumsy in his attempt to free the U.S. diplomatic hostages trapped in Tehran after the fall of Mohammad Reza Pahlavi, the shah of Iran, and in responding to the buildup of Russian nuclear force aimed at Europe. He also supported cutting the defense budget.

Despite his moralistic approach to foreign affairs, Carter chose a traditional political realist to be his national security adviser, Zbigniew Brzezinski. Brzezinski spent part of his early youth in Hitler's Germany and Stalin's Soviet Union, where his father was posted as a Polish diplomat. He once remarked of World War II, "The extraordinary violence that was perpetrated against Poland did affect my perception of the world, and made me much more sensitive to the fact that a great deal of world politics is a fundamental struggle."[2]

While Brzezinski had a good personal rapport with Carter, he considered the president to be naïve about the realities of world politics: "Unlike Kissinger, who had in Nixon a clear ally in shaping a grand strategy for the country," he wrote, "I have to do it through indirection." Brzezinski tried to educate Carter about the realities of power politics; he recalled telling the president, "'Before you are a President Wilson you have to be a few years a President Truman.' By that I meant that the President first had to convince the American public and the world of his toughness, and only then, during his second term, could he adopt a more Wilsonian approach."[3] Carter, for his part, wrote that he and Brzezinski "had many arguments about history, politics, international events, and foreign policy—often disagreeing strongly and fundamentally."[4]

These differences were most starkly visible over Iran policy. While Brzezinski was always a strong supporter of the shah of Iran, Carter was somewhat ambivalent. During his first meeting with the shah in 1977, Carter publicly expressed support for him but privately recommended that he ease up on police actions against the Iranian opposition; Carter also cut back on U.S. arms sales to Iran. Carter's approach created uncertainty in the shah's mind about what Washington really wanted and reminded the monarch of what he perceived as President Kennedy's attempt to ease him out of power during widespread political unrest in Iran in 1963.[5]

As political unrest spread again in Iran in late 1978, Brzezinski tried without success to convince Carter to encourage the shah to use the Iranian military to crack down on the growing protests. Energy Secretary James Schlesinger and Defense Secretary Harold Brown shared Brzezinski's view, although Brown wanted to defer the crackdown to some unspecified future time and Schlesinger was not a major participant in policy deliberations on Iran. A crackdown probably would have resulted in the deaths of several thousand religious and student political activists. Ironically, many of the religious activists would go on to kill or exile the students in the Iranian civil war during the early 1980s.

The State Department favored less confrontational options. Carter's secretary of state, Cyrus Vance, wanted to persuade the shah to cobble together a broad coalition civilian government and to avoid a crackdown at all costs. The U.S. ambassador in Iran, William Sullivan, who had no background in Iranian affairs, wanted the U.S. government to reach out to the Iranian opposition, including Ayatollah Ruhollah Khomeini, who was living in exile in Paris. The Iran office at the State Department, headed by Foreign Service Officer Henry Precht, wanted the United States to urge the shah to abandon his throne and choose exile. Faced with this array of options, Carter would invariably end up pursuing an ineffective middle path, telling the shah that the United States would support him in whatever action he chose, rather than encouraging him to go in any particular direction.

Behind these differences lay fundamental contrasts in political worldviews. Brzezinski stressed the importance of U.S. interests and what he perceived as Iranian interests and was willing to countenance bloodshed to keep the shah in power, given the importance of a friendly Iran. In contrast, Carter and Vance placed a higher premium on moral considerations and refused to urge the shah to crack down. Brzezinski was also more wary of dramatic political change; Carter, and even more his State Department advisers, were less so (an attitude recalling the optimism of Jefferson toward the French Revolution).[6]

Protests against the shah's regime had been taking place in Iran periodically since the early 1960s for a variety of reasons. Politically, the shah failed to co-opt enough of the Iranian middle classes into a more inclusive political system. His economic modernization policies, such as the creation of a modern banking system, increased prosperity but also put many local money changers out of business. Socially, the shah alienated religious conservatives by supporting the rights of women and religious minorities and maintaining a lavish lifestyle. Both the shah and many Western observers failed to understand that modernization, while generally good for a country in the longer run, often creates instability in the shorter term.[7]

The wave of political unrest that would drive the shah from power began in earnest in August 1978, when a fire, the cause of which remains uncertain, killed several hundred spectators in a cinema in the city of Abadan. Protesters blamed the shah, and military conscripts killed scores of protesters on September 8 in Tehran.

U.S. leaders, however, did not focus on the crisis initially for several reasons. Consumed with the Camp David talks between Egypt and Israel, they were told by the U.S. intelligence community that the shah would crack down on the demonstrators if he truly felt under threat. However, U.S. intelligence was unaware that the shah was dying of cancer and was not his normal self. Moreover, he never had been the ruthless tyrant that the Western press had made him out to be—a reputation that he himself had cultivated and that Soviet propaganda played up for gullible audiences in Europe and North America. The shah in fact was rather indecisive by nature. He had fled the country during the 1953 unrest under Prime Minister Mohammad Mosaddegh; he had refused to give orders to fire on demonstrators during the political unrest of 1963 (after which he spared Khomeini's life); and he had turned down Saddam Hussein's offer to kill Khomeini when the latter was in exile in Iraq. The shah had inherited his father's throne but not his ruthlessness.

In early October 1978, the shah told Ambassador Sullivan that his generals were urging him to crack down to preempt the spread of political unrest to his troops. In late October Sullivan cabled Washington that the embassy opposed any crowd-control devices and any high-level visits from Washington in order to avoid the United States being too closely associated with the shah. The State Department felt the United States should be seen to be a neutral outsider that could work with all parties, including the religious ones. State also believed incorrectly that there were enough pro-American elements in Iran to avoid a disaster in case the shah did fall.

As a foreign policy realist, Brzezinski, was instinctively wary of revolutionary change. In his memoirs he cites the most famous book on revolutions in American academe, Crane Brinton's *The Anatomy of Revolution*, which takes a pessimistic view of the political chaos and violence often unleashed by political upheaval.[8] Brzezinski's priority was to keep the shah in power, which could only be accomplished, he felt, by the shah ordering the military to crack down on the protesters and then reaching out to broaden his base of support. "In my view," he wrote, "a policy of conciliation and concessions might have worked, had it been adopted two or three years earlier, before the crisis reached a politically acute stage. . . . But once the crisis had become a contest of will and power, advocacy of compromise and conciliation simply played into the hands of those determined to effect a complete revolution."[9]

Brzezinski called the shah on November 3 and told him that the United States would support him in whatever he did and that Brzezinski himself thought that "concessions alone are likely to produce a more and more explosive situation." Significantly, the Iranian monarch asked Brzezinski to repeat the phrase that a concessions-only policy was counterproductive to make sure that he had understood what Washington was recommending. The shah also asked if the U.S. ambassador had been briefed about the message since Brzezinski's advice was at variance with Sullivan's.[10]

On November 9 Sullivan cabled Washington that it should probably begin to think about an Iran without the shah, which was probably the ambassador's way of expressing his desire for the monarch to leave the country. He opined that Ayatollah Khomeini would probably return to Tehran as part of an agreement with the pro-Western military and would play a "Gandhi-like role" in Iranian politics.[11]

During December the Iranian monarch continued to oscillate between strong appeals to Sullivan for American support and complaints about the lack of such support; between predictions of his own impending downfall and dire warnings that the military was about to stage a bloodbath to prevent it. Sullivan merely repeated that the shah should do what he thought best and avoided encouraging him to use the military to defend his throne.

Back in Washington, Brzezinski felt he could not push too aggressively for a military takeover because "the very notion of initiating such a coup from Washington went so much against the grain of the dominant values in the White House and State Department." Instead, he had to argue somewhat disingenuously that a military government might be the best chance to avoid a bloody civil war and that it should therefore be considered as a last resort: "That, in turn, made it easier for Vance, [Deputy Secretary of State Warren] Christopher and others to counter that the time to move towards a drastic solution had not yet come." Carter turned aside Brzezinski's suggestion in mid-December that Brzezinski or Secretary of Energy Schlesinger travel to Tehran to strengthen the shah's resolve.[12]

During the first two weeks of January, Brzezinski made his final attempts to convince Carter to call the Iranian monarch and urge him to resort to a military crackdown. According to Brzezinski's diary notes from a long meeting with Carter on January 3:

> When I went in to talk to the President at 6 p.m. with the cables, I also told him that I felt we were not doing enough and that this could backfire very gravely. He was rather irritated and asked me what I wished to have done. I told him that we should have encouraged the military to stage a coup. He told me that we couldn't do this, not only because of the [historical] record but also because there is no military leader we could identify who would lead such a coup. He has a point in a specific sense, but my view is that we do not have to identify a leader. What we need to do is to give a clearer signal and a leader will emerge.[13]

On January 4, Brzezinski, whose advice was increasingly getting on Carter's nerves, warned the president that "unfortunately, world politics was not a kindergarten and that we had to consider also what will be the longer-range costs if the military failed to act."[14]

The shah's departure from Iran on January 16 proved to be the final blow to the morale of the Iranian military and the beginning of the end of the pro-Western regime. The administration sent over a senior U.S. military commander, General Robert Huyser, then deputy U.S. commander in Europe, in an unsuccessful attempt to buck up the morale of the Iranian military. Huyser reported to Washington that the new Iranian prime minister, Shapur Bakhtiar, wanted to arrest Khomeini upon his imminent return to Iran. Brzezinski and

Brown wanted to encourage Bakhtiar to move forward; Vance, always the dove, objected strenuously in part because Khomeini might be killed. Carter eventually approved a modified message favored by Brzezinski and Brown. However, Bakhtiar's government soon collapsed and Khomeini returned on January 31.[15]

With the departure of the shah, the next policy debate focused on whether the United States should provide exile to the Iranian monarch. Initially, all senior officials favored that option, but Vance edged away from it to avoid provoking the new regime. Brzezinski felt, in more classical security terms, that the United States should stand by its long-term partners to demonstrate that friends could count on the United States. Similarly, former secretary of state Henry Kissinger lobbied the administration privately and publicly, criticizing it for treating the shah, in Kissinger's words, as a Wagnerian Flying Dutchman, doomed to roam the earth in search of a haven.[16] Carter tended to side with Vance and against Brzezinski. In October 1979, however, the U.S. government learned that the shah had cancer. At this point, the State Department recommended that he leave Mexico, his temporary abode, and be allowed to come to the United States for medical treatment, but only if the Iranian government approved. Carter decided simply to inform the Iranian government that the shah would enter the United States for medical treatment in late October. Carter seemed to want the shah to leave as soon as possible, and at one point he hung up on Brzezinski after accusing him of conspiring with Kissinger to keep the Iranian monarch in the United States.[17]

Iranian radicals took over the U.S. embassy in November, ostensibly in reaction to the entry of the shah to the United States. While they asserted their goal was to force the United States to send the former monarch back to Iran for a trial and execution, something they knew would not happen, their real goal was to create a superheated political atmosphere to isolate their more moderate rivals, who were still running most of the Iranian government. The shah left the United States for Panama in mid-December 1979, and when he died in Cairo in July 1980, it made little difference to the student activists and religious radicals. For them, the shah had always been a means rather than an end.

The administration's inept response to the embassy takeover reflected a lack of understanding of an admittedly complex political situation and its political desperation with the approach of the November 1980 election. Initially, the differences among Carter's policy advisers mirrored the disagreements that divided them about whether to urge the shah to crack down or not. Brzezinski wanted to use military force, perhaps taking Kharg Island in the lower Persian Gulf, where many of the Iranian oil facilities were located. For this hardboiled realist, the United States' reputation was more important than the lives of the hostages because countries gear their policies around reputation. Vance generally opposed any military retaliation because the hostages' lives were his top priority. Carter was somewhere in the middle; he wanted some form of military retaliation, but he was concerned about its dangers to the hostages.

In December 1979 the administration failed to understand an important new development, the Soviet invasion of Afghanistan. Brzezinski believed that uniting the Islamic world behind an effort to expel the Soviets from Afghanistan should be the top priority and that an attack on Iran would push Tehran toward the Soviets. However, as a Soviet specialist, Brzezinski knew relatively little about the nuances of the Middle East, and Carter and Vance understood even less. Their assumption that Iran would be needed for the anti-Soviet coalition in Afghanistan was wrong. Iran would play a small role in the successful effort to encourage a Soviet withdrawal, unlike Pakistan and Saudi Arabia. Moreover, the administration's assumption that a military attack on a religious Iran would drive it toward the Soviet atheists was also wrong, given the historic rivalries between the two civilizations. This rivalry began to decline significantly only after the collapse of the Soviet Union, which meant that the two countries no longer shared a common border and Moscow was therefore no longer an immediate threat to Tehran.

The United States could have pursued the option of a naval blockade of Iran's oil exports. This would have applied pressure on Tehran without killing any Iranians or necessarily endangering the hostages. It would also have helped dispel the growing impression of American weakness in the region that Egyptian president Anwar Sadat had warned Carter about in the spring of 1980. In contrast, the alternative adopted in April, the special operations raid, smacked of political desperation. The distances that the helicopters would have to fly were huge, the intelligence about the whereabouts of the hostages was uncertain, and the weather conditions were unpredictable. It was not surprising that the operation aborted in the desert.

In fairness to Carter, it would have been difficult for anyone to grasp fully the disaster that Khomeini's coming to power would represent. Nonetheless, a more seasoned president, or at least a bolder one such as Nixon, might have accepted Brzezinski's advice in favor of military intervention to try to save the shah. However, Carter was a Wilsonian moralist who was generally critical of U.S. interventions in the politics of foreign countries.

Ironically, the fall of the shah resulted in a staggering blow to the human rights that Carter had championed. Soon after Khomeini's return to Iran in January 1979, political executions by religious conservatives began. The first targets were Iranian military officials, and then the focus shifted to the political opposition, as well as women accused of "honor" crimes. The religious government established an investigative body to expose the shah's political crimes, but since the investigators found fewer than two hundred political prisoners killed over three decades, the regime quietly terminated the study. According to one U.S. academic, more than double that number of Iranian dissidents were killed in Iranian jails during one week in July 1988.[18]

Again, in fairness to Carter, there was no guarantee that a military crackdown would have succeeded in keeping the shah in power and protesters did eventually overwhelm the army after the shah left the country in January 1979. Yet the army remained largely intact until then. In September 1978, for example, Iranian troops obeyed orders and fired on protesters at Jaleh Square in Tehran, killing several hundred. In November 1978 the opposition initially drew back from confrontation after the shah appointed a new government headed by the Iranian chief of staff, the mild-mannered General Gholamreza Azhari. Protesters became aggressive again after they realized that Azhari, acting under the shah's orders, was not going to order a military crackdown.[19]

If a crackdown had succeeded in keeping the shah in power, enabling him to pass the throne to his son, it is likely there would have been no Iran-Iraq War, which led to the first Gulf War, which in turn led to the second U.S. invasion of Iraq, which resulted in the rise of the Islamic State in Iraq. Moreover, there would have been no hostile Iranian nuclear weapons program and repressive religious regime.

Just as the French Revolution plunged Europe into a quarter century of war, the fall of the shah resulted in a series of wars and the deaths of millions in the region. Whether a different U.S. foreign policy could have prevented his fall is an open question. However, the debates among Carter, Brzezinski, Vance, and Sullivan display a representative range of views of how political leaders react to the tensions between interests and values as the basis of foreign policy. Brzezinski's priority was U.S. interests, as embodied by the shah's survival. Carter and Vance favored values, specifically the avoidance of bloodshed and any traces of U.S. intervention. Half a century later, the repercussions of the shah's fall continue.

CHAPTER 9

George H. W. Bush and the First Gulf War

The Diplomacy of Determination

President George H. W. Bush, like Theodore Roosevelt and Richard Nixon, was more interested in foreign policy than in domestic issues. Like Nixon, Bush benefited from an excellent foreign policy background as vice president, CIA director, and U.S. representative to China. His principal foreign policy adviser, Brent Scowcroft, who had been Henry Kissinger's deputy, ran what is widely considered the best-managed post–World War II foreign policy team in the second half of the twentieth century.[1]

Bush and Scowcroft would put all their foreign policy experience to good use in the first Gulf War. The war went so well that its success is almost taken for granted, but at the time there were no guarantees of success against one of the largest armies in the world, and one with combat experience in the Iran-Iraq War. Most congressional Democrats, U.S. military commanders, and European leaders wanted to avoid hostilities and favored economic sanctions to attempt to force Saddam to withdraw from Kuwait. The congressional authorization to use armed force to expel Saddam (passed 52–47 in the Senate and 250–183 in the House) was the narrowest such vote in U.S. history, aside from the War of 1812.

Bush demonstrated two key attributes of successful statecraft. First, he understood the complexities of the diplomatic and military situation that faced him with the Iraqi annexation of Kuwait. And he displayed a single-minded determination to expel Iraqi troops once he had concluded that economic sanctions would be inadequate.

The Iraqi invasion of Kuwait caught the United States and the world by surprise on August 1, 1990. The CIA and the U.S. Central Command (CENTCOM), the military command in charge of the Middle East, had thought that Saddam might take the disputed Rumalia oil field along the Iraq-Kuwait border, but not all of Kuwait. Arab leaders had assured Bush that Saddam would not invade.[2]

Initially, there was no consensus at senior levels of the U.S. government about how to react to the invasion. At the first senior meeting, Scowcroft stated he was "frankly appalled at the undertone of the discussion, which suggested resignation to the invasion and even adaptation to a *fait accompli*. There was a huge gap between those who saw what was happening as the major crisis of our time and those who treated it as the *crisis du jour*."[3] On the hawkish side were Bush, Scowcroft, and Defense Secretary Richard Cheney; the doves included Secretary of State James Baker, Chairman of the Joint Chiefs of Staff Colin Powell, and CENTCOM commander Norman Schwarzkopf.

Baker, Powell, and Schwarzkopf seemed inclined to defend only Saudi Arabia and write off Kuwait. Baker, a close friend of Bush and a political operative more than a foreign policy authority, worried that the war would hurt the administration's reputation with the U.S. public. Powell and Schwarzkopf reflected the risk-averse nature of much of the U.S. military since the Vietnam War, a tendency reinforced by the humanitarian intervention debacle in Lebanon in the early 1980s under President Ronald Reagan. In addition, while the air force was more optimistic about the prospects for military success with its new arsenal of precision weapons, Powell and Schwarzkopf came from the more skittish army.

Despite these misgivings by the U.S. military, Bush set the tone at the second meeting: the invasion was a major challenge to the international order and would not be tolerated. At stake were the security of the Gulf, the sanctity of international borders more generally, and the credibility of the United States.[4]

The immediate problem for Bush and Scowcroft to overcome was Saudi Arabia's questioning of U.S. resolve. In early August, Saudi ambassador Prince Bandar bin Sultan, King Fahd's favorite nephew, told Scowcroft that the United States "did not exactly have a reputation in the region for reliability." He gave two examples. In 1979 the United States, under President Carter, had offered a squadron of F-15s to Saudi Arabia as a gesture of support after the shah's departure, only to announce on their way that they were unarmed. Similarly, the United States abandoned Lebanon in 1984 after the murderous attacks on the marine barracks. Moreover, King Fahd was noncommittal about inviting U.S. military forces to defend his country in his first telephone call with Bush. However, the Defense Department's subsequent briefings on its plans to send several hundred thousand troops to the region convinced the Saudis that this president, unlike Carter and Reagan, was deadly serious. These initial briefings focused on the defense of Saudi Arabia; plans to liberate Kuwait would come only later.[5]

Bush also faced a more general problem. The international community generally supported, or at least was not opposed to, sending troops to defend Saudi Arabia, but it shied away from trying to liberate Kuwait. Most Arab and European leaders, and Soviet secretary general Mikhail Gorbachev, told Bush that the international community should opt for an indefinite period of economic sanctions, mainly a boycott of Iraqi oil, and seek unspecified compromises to avoid war. Arab leaders were concerned that war would provoke political unrest in their own countries; the USSR opposed an attack on its former Iraqi partner; and nearly everyone feared higher oil prices in the wake of hostilities.

Bush also had to contend with the spectacle of Western leaders, including German chancellor Helmut Kohl, former president Jimmy Carter, and former British prime minister Edward Heath, visiting Baghdad to counsel Saddam to show flexibility. Bush and Scowcroft knew that Saddam would interpret such efforts as signs of weakness, which would only strengthen his resolve to remain in Kuwait. The only true international hawk outside the Gulf states and Israel was British prime minister Margaret Thatcher, a force of nature, who warned that the West must enforce international norms against aggression.

Bush and Scowcroft concluded quickly that economic sanctions were an exercise in wishful thinking, reminiscent of Jefferson's hope that economic coercion would change British maritime policy. The international community had agreed to stop buying Iraqi oil, but Saddam could always smuggle out significant amounts via Iraq's long borders with Iran, Jordan, Turkey, and Syria. Saddam and the Iraqi elite would also be largely insulated from the most serious impact of economic sanctions. Finally, as former secretary of state Henry Kissinger pointed out in congressional hearings, Saudi Arabia could not tolerate a large number of foreign, and particularly Western, military forces on its territory indefinitely. Time therefore favored Iraq.[6] Moreover, a perceptive Bush felt that there was a reasonable chance of U.S. military success at an acceptable cost because Iraq, in spite of its large army, had performed in a relatively mediocre fashion against Iran in the 1980s Iran-Iraq War. This was more like a World War I army than a modern one.[7]

Bush's skepticism about economic sanctions was strengthened by the fact that Saddam showed no signs of interest in withdrawing from what he had declared to be a new Iraqi province. Slowly, the international community was coming around to the idea that perhaps military force would be needed to expel Saddam. Bush therefore brought matters to a head on October 30 at a meeting with senior advisers to discuss whether to send additional military forces to expel the Iraqis from Kuwait, not just to defend Saudi Arabia. Bush was determined to pursue the military option despite the U.S. military's forecast of about five thousand deaths. Secretary of State Powell recounts that he told Bush the following at the meeting: "We're approaching two hundred and fifty thousand for the defensive phase [defending Saudi Arabia]. But if the president opts for this offensive, we'll need a hell of lot more. How much more Scowcroft asked. Nearly double, I said. About another two hundred thousand troops. Whew, Scowcroft said, his gasp echoed by others around the room. I glanced at the President. He had not blinked. Okay, do it, he said."[8]

According to his biographer, Scowcroft wondered if the joint chiefs had set their requirements so high to discourage Bush from attempting to expel Saddam. Conversely, the military may simply have wanted to err on the side of caution, whatever its private doubts about the mission. Bush wanted to give the military what it asked for in part to eliminate the possibility of leaks from disgruntled officers.[9]

Bush and Scowcroft displayed not just determination, but also political insight about their war aims. They did not want Saddam to withdraw his forces and keep them just across the border in Iraq, thereby terrifying the Kuwaitis and intimidating the rest of the Gulf. Saddam's troops must either withdraw or be driven back into the country's interior, where they had been based before the crisis. Moreover, Bush and Scowcroft wanted to destroy as much as possible of the Republican Guard, Iraq's elite military force. Finally, Saddam was to be seen as having lost decisively so that he could never claim that he had battled the West to a draw. A decisive defeat would drive home to the Iraqi people and military that such an invasion should never be attempted again.

At the same time, the regular Iraqi army should not be destroyed to the point where it could not defend Iraq from a more powerful Iran. Ideally, someone from the regular army might emerge out of a military defeat to overthrow Saddam. Hence, determination and cunning were combined in war aims.[10]

In the face of Saddam's continued refusal to withdraw troops, the international coalition air war, consisting of U.S. and European forces, began in mid-January. Yet even then, Soviet secretary general Gorbachev, along with France and Egypt, urged Bush to suspend the air attacks to encourage Saddam to withdraw. Bush told his team that he did not like the idea but did not want to undermine the coalition or reject outright the advice of Gorbachev, who had largely backed his efforts. The president told Gorbachev that the United States would not fire on retreating Iraqis if they chose to withdraw immediately. Saddam blundered yet again by turning down the Soviet proposal—to the relief of the Bush team. Bush had suggested earlier to Gorbachev that the Soviets should send military forces to join the coalition, though Scowcroft was relieved when Gorbachev turned down the proposal, as U.S. officials had anticipated. Bush, reflecting his foreign policy sophistication, understood that Gorbachev's opposition to the war was related in part to his desire to minimize the prospects of unrest among his own large Muslim population.[11]

On February 24 the coalition's ground forces began their five-day rout of Iraqi forces. Saddam proposed to negotiate their withdrawal even as his terrified troops fled Kuwait.[12] At this point, Bush made perhaps his only major mistake. He and all his senior advisers assumed mistakenly that the Republican Guard had been largely destroyed in the devastation of the five-day ground war. According to Chairman Powell, Schwarzkopf initially reported overwhelming military success, though he called back to say that some Republican Guard units might have slipped away: "Although we [Bush and his advisers] were all taken slightly aback, no one felt that what we had heard changed the basic equation. The back of the Iraqi army had been broken. What was left of it was retreating north. There was no need to fight a battle of annihilation."[13]

Moreover, according to Scowcroft, "We had all become increasingly concerned over impressions being created in the press about the 'highway of death' from Kuwait City to Basra."[14] This was, after all, the first war when combat footage was broadcast nonstop over television.

In fact, coalition forces had destroyed several Republican Guard divisions but not all of them because the ground attack had gone so well that most of the guard in the Baghdad region did not have time to join the battle. They were in Baghdad to protect Saddam from a military coup and probably to ensure that the regular army would fight against the international coalition. In short, Bush and his senior advisers got caught up in the "euphoria in the air," to cite Scowcroft, and opted for an early cease-fire when several more days or a week of combat, even if only in the air, could have inflicted more serious damage on Saddam's main power base.[15]

Despite Saddam's survival, the Gulf War was in many ways a major achievement. The U.S.-led coalition had defeated Saddam decisively, thereby ensuring the independence of the smaller Gulf countries. The victory had also strengthened America's diplomatic and military prestige in general.

Bush's management of the war demonstrated several key attributes of effective statecraft. He understood the complex situation facing him. Chairman Powell, for example, noted that Bush understood the international oil market and its policy implications better than any of his advisers. Bush also correctly sensed that the oil boycott would not force Saddam to withdraw from Kuwait. He also realized that for all its huge size, the Iraqi army had fought in a mediocre fashion during the Iran-Iraq War.[16]

Additionally, Bush was adept at working with international colleagues. As a gregarious political leader and former vice president, he had a fund of relationships that he had cultivated over the years to call upon. He felt, for example, that one important reason that French president François Mitterrand was cooperative during the crisis, despite the standoffish attitude of his foreign ministry and the opposition of his defense minister, was that Bush had invited the French president to his home in Kennebunkport early in his presidency. He handled Gorbachev with tact, although they were working at cross-purposes much of the time. Even before the war, Bush had reached out to leaders who might not necessarily be of much help to him as president; within the first year of his presidency, he had called every leader in Latin America. Many of these contacts came in handy during the war.

Perhaps the most impressive of Bush's character traits was his single-minded determination to expel Saddam regardless of the risk to his presidency. Bush could have accepted Iraq's annexation of Kuwait and drawn the line at Saudi Arabia. U.S. public opinion would not have forced him to liberate Kuwait. Yet, according to his senior aide Robert Gates, Bush said privately that he would either expel Iraq from Kuwait or be impeached. Gates and other U.S. officials believed Bush would have invaded Kuwait even if he had lost the congressional votes authorizing the use of force.[17]

That determination was best expressed, as noted by Chairman Powell, at Bush's October 30 meeting with his advisers. According to Deputy National Security Adviser Robert Gates, Bush demonstrated the same determination when he met with the heads of the U.S. military services the same day. Gates quotes a military briefer's words to the president: "You'll need Seventh Corps out of Germany, heart of NATO's defense. Six carrier groups, a week before midterm elections, and oh, and you'll have to activate both the National Guard and the Reserves. In other words, you're going to reach into every community in America and take people away from their homes and jobs." According to Gates, "Bush pushed his chair back, stood up, looked at Cheney and said, 'You got it, let me know if you need more,' and walked out of the room. Cheney's jaw dropped. Powell's jaw dropped. Cheney looked at Scowcroft and says, 'Does he know what he just authorized?' And Brent smiled and he said, 'He knows perfectly well what he authorized.'"[18]

With Bush as the last World War II veteran to serve as president, it was a fitting valedictory tribute that someone from his generation would lead the United States to its most decisive military victory since the war that he had fought in half a century before.

CHAPTER 10

Obama

The Reluctant Foreign Policy President

When President Barack Obama entered the Oval Office, he replaced Winston Churchill's bust with that of Martin Luther King Jr., a telling symbol of his priorities. Obama's first secretary of defense, Robert Gates, noted that Obama's heart never seemed to be in military affairs:

> One quality I missed in Obama was passion, especially when it came to the two wars [in Iraq and Afghanistan]. In my presence, [George W.] Bush—very unlike his father—was pretty unsentimental. But he was passionate about the war in Iraq; on occasion, at a Medal of Honor ceremony or the like, I would see his eyes well up with tears. I worked for Obama longer than Bush, and I never saw his eyes well up.... the only military matter, apart from leaks, about which I ever sensed deep passion on his part was "Don't Ask, Don't Tell." For him, changing the laws seemed to be the inevitable next step in the civil rights movement.[1]

Obama's former CIA director and defense secretary Leon Panetta noted a similar lack of intensity, at least about international affairs.[2]

Obama's major interests were domestic affairs. After the successful special forces raid that killed Bin Laden, the president mused about why the country could not devote the same kind of energy to overcoming American's domestic challenges. His main foreign policy goal was "not to do stupid stuff," in his own words.[3]

Strong interest in foreign affairs does not guarantee success, but its absence is likely to result in mixed results at best. Regarding the two wars he inherited from President George W. Bush, Obama acquiesced to senior military commanders' request for more troops for Afghanistan, doubling the U.S. military commitment from fifty thousand to one hundred thousand. In retrospect at least, he should have begun to withdraw troops from Afghanistan, not add to them, given the waning domestic support for the commitment and intelligence reporting about a lack of military progress. In Iraq President Obama withdrew all U.S. military forces in 2011 and 2012, despite warnings that the Iraqi army would not be able to stand on its own. The decision contributed to the rise of the Islamic State in Iraq and forced Obama to send back about the same number of military forces that he had withdrawn.[4]

In 2014 Obama refused to send lethal weapons to Ukraine in response to the Russian annexation of Crimea and invasion of eastern Ukraine. Russian president Vladimir Putin saw this as an admission that the United States did not care that much and Russia had little to fear. In 2016 Obama only admonished Moscow with modest verbal declarations about its interference in the U.S. election when he could have at least expelled the Russian ambassador.

To his credit, Obama was the first American president to take climate change seriously, and he promoted the abortive Indo-Pacific free-trade agreement, which a protectionist Congress and President Donald Trump turned against. Moreover, Obama presided over the 2011 raid against Bin Laden, and he reached the 2015 diplomatic agreement to suspend Iran's nuclear weapons program. In short, Obama had several important international achievements, but traditional security issues involving armed conflict were not his major interest or strong suit.

For the purposes of our study, we will examine in detail two cases during the Obama administration that demonstrate the president's failure to anticipate events and his reticence about the uses of military force. The first involves the U.S./NATO intervention in Libya in 2011, which Obama himself acknowledged did not work out well. The second incident involves the president's awkward response to the Syrian regime's use of chemical weapons in 2013, the red-line incident. His lack of affinity for military affairs, as noted by his defense secretaries Gates, Panetta, and Ash Carter, recalls the uncertainties and tentativeness of Presidents Thomas Jefferson and Jimmy Carter.

One cannot blame poor advice for Obama's mistakes in these cases. During the 2011 NATO intervention, the president benefited from the counsel of Gates, a moderate Republican, whom Obama had kept on from the Bush administration. During the 2013 Syrian red-line incident, Obama also got good advice from Carter, a seasoned defense intellectual, and from Vice President Joe Biden and Secretary of State John Kerry, who had both served on the Senate Foreign Relations Committee. Thus, Obama, to his credit, sought out advice from seasoned foreign policy exports.

At the same time, the president surrounded himself on his personal staff with young amateurs from his Senate office, his political campaign, or academia. They were generally wary of military force except perhaps for humanitarian purposes. Obama generally sided with these young and inexperienced staff members over his more experienced advisers.[5]

Obama's uncertain foreign policy touch was apparent when political unrest broke out in the Middle East in early 2011, the so-called Arab Spring. All of Obama's senior advisers, including Secretary of State Hillary Clinton, Gates, and Biden, advised the president to be prudent and not urge Egyptian president Hosni Mubarak to leave office because it would create a vacuum that the Muslim Brotherhood, the main opposition group, could fill. Moreover, these advisers felt that encouraging Mubarak to leave would send a message to international partners that the United States was an unreliable ally.

Obama, however, sided with his young political advisers who supported a democracy agenda, as had the inexperienced George W. Bush, and the president telephoned Mubarak to urge him to leave office. It would not be the last time that Obama sided with his young, less experienced operatives, whose lack of knowledge and naiveté constantly astonished Gates: "But how can anyone know which is the right or wrong side of history when nearly all revolutions, begun with hope and idealism, culminate in repression and bloodshed? After Mubarak, what?"[6]

True to the senior advisers' fears, Mubarak resigned in February 2011 and Islamists quickly filled the vacuum. In fall parliamentary elections, the Muslim Brotherhood won 47 percent of the seats and the ultraconservative Islamist Salafist party 25 percent. The brotherhood then reneged on its promise not to present a candidate for the presidency and ran Mohammed Morsi, who won a narrow victory over a former air force general in June 2012. Yet the Egyptian people turned out in massive numbers to demonstrate in favor of Morsi's departure within a year of his election as the Egyptian economy plunged into chaos, caused by a combination of Morsi's incompetence and the military's sabotage. The Egyptian military therefore was more than happy to remove Morsi in 2013. Egypt had survived the near-death experience about which Gates and other senior advisers had warned Obama.

During the same period, the political uprising in Libya and the fall of President Muammar al-Qaddafi in 2011 presented another example of a lack of prudence and a well-intentioned policy gone wrong. Most of Obama's senor advisers, and Defense Secretary Gates in particular, opposed military intervention because they felt that no major U.S. interests were at stake. During March 2011 Gates made no fewer than six public statements against military intervention. He argued that the U.S. military was already overstretched in Iraq and Afghanistan and that no one knew much about the Libyan opposition. He also asked about the lack of post-conflict planning. The difficulties of intervention and lack of such planning in Iraq and Afghanistan offered reasons for major concern.[7]

However, Obama's more inexperienced advisers, including National Security Adviser Susan Rice, U.S. Ambassador to the United Nations Samantha Power, and presidential aide Ben Rhodes, urged him to prevent a massacre as Qaddafi's forces closed in on Benghazi, the center of the rebellion and the country's second-largest city. At the same time, well-educated Libyan opposition leaders, many of whom had not lived in Libya for years, met with Secretary of State Clinton and other Western leaders and offered soothing reassurances concerning the Libyan opposition movement.

In fairness to Obama, French president Nicolas Sarkozy and British prime minister David Cameron were also urging a NATO intervention; even the Arab League voted in favor of military force to protect Benghazi. Many European and Arab leaders, and Obama himself, believed, incorrectly, that the Arab Spring was the wave of the future. Moreover, Obama probably reasoned privately that he could avoid domestic political damage as long as he limited military intervention to aerial attacks against Qaddafi's forces. As a result, the president sided with Secretary of State Clinton, who joined Obama's junior advisers to recommend military intervention to protect Benghazi at an internal meeting on March 15.

In contrast, Gates continued to oppose yet another U.S. military engagement: "[Congressional] hearings were awkward for me because many of the members were raising precisely the concerns I had raised during the internal administration debates. Asked if the situation in Libya involved our 'vital national interests,' I honestly said I did not think so—but our closest allies felt that it affected their vital interests and therefore we had an obligation to help them."[8]

This was probably the best reply that Gates could give since the United States had no particular interest in replacing Qaddafi. In fact, the Libyan leader had begun to moderate his behavior after challenging the West during the 1970s and 1980s. Beginning in the 1990s and 2000s, he had stopped terrorist attacks on Western targets, provided financial compensation to families who had lost family members in past attacks, and abandoned his chemical weapons and rudimentary nuclear program. Moreover, while Qaddafi continued to be a repressive leader, he never engaged in repression on the scale of Iraq's Saddam Hussein or Syria's Assad family.

Gates also correctly anticipated future dangers. He feared that once Western countries intervened to prevent Qaddafi's attacks on Benghazi, they would likely be dragged toward removing him altogether; otherwise, he would resume his assault on Benghazi at any time, including during the night to avoid air attacks. To protect Benghazi, then, might not NATO have to try to push Qaddafi's forces back toward Tripoli and establish some kind of line in the sand between the two cities, an indefinite commitment?

Moreover, administration officials failed to anticipate additional dangers of military intervention, including discussing the potential negative repercussions of ousting Qaddafi altogether, a policy that they would slide into.[9] Such a discussion might have included the likely emergence of terrorism in the chaos of a civil war; in fact, the Islamic State would emerge for a time and terrorists would murder U.S. Ambassador Chris Stevens in 2012. They might also have warned about the danger of the losing side in a Libyan civil war fleeing the country and destabilizing Mali, as happened. They did not foresee the increase of illegal migration into Europe that occurred during the prolonged civil war after Qaddafi's fall in 2011. Finally, Russia, which opposed military intervention, became even more difficult to deal with elsewhere, including Syria.[10]

In addition, Islamists in the Middle East and Africa could benefit from the dispersal of the Libyan army's arms inventory. Finally, unless an intervention resulted in a clear success, it would reduce the willingness of Obama and the American electorate to intervene in the future where the stakes could be more important. (His dovishness over Syria was due reportedly in part to the imbroglio in Libya.)[11]

Perhaps this lack of prudence by the United States and other NATO countries was best reflected in the following exchange between the British parliamentary inquiry and British chief of the defense staff Lord David Richards. When asked if NATO knew that the head of al-Qaeda in North Africa, Abdelhakim Belhaj, was participating in the anti-Qaddafi uprising. Richards replied, "Respectable Libyans were assuring the Foreign Office that militant Islamists would not benefit from the uprising [and that] with the benefit of hindsight that was wishful thinking at best."[12]

Even from the perspective of humanitarian concerns, the Libyan intervention proved a failure. Qaddafi's forces gained the upper hand against the armed opposition within a month of the outbreak of hostilities and were on the verge of retaking Benghazi by March 18 when NATO intervened. While Qaddafi's forces would surely have been brutal toward the armed opposition in Benghazi, those deaths would have paled in comparison with the carnage of the ensuing years of civil war.[13]

Nor did the Libyan leaders of the ensuing civil war seem particularly committed to political reform and human rights; leaders who must kill their way to the top usually are not. In contrast, the U.S. and other Western governments did know in 2011 that Saif Qaddafi, the second son and heir apparent of his father, seemed open to the prospects of political and economic reform. Whether he would have been able, and ultimately willing, to move in those directions will never be known. However, he would have been an improvement over his father and perhaps over Libya's civil war leaders.[14]

Ironically, Russia and Turkey would emerge as more influential countries in Libya than the United States after Qaddafi's fall. Russia subsequently backed General Khalifa Haftar's forces based in Benghazi, including with the Wagner Group special forces; Turkey would became the principal backer of the Tripoli-based faction. As much as Putin had opposed Western intervention in Libya, perhaps he had the last laugh.

Obama lost interest in Libya quickly and returned to his priority, domestic politics. He gave a speech at the National Defense University in late March 2011 declaring that regime change was not the U.S. goal and then said little thereafter, as NATO and U.S. forces would help the opposition to overthrow Qaddafi. Secretary of State Clinton chuckled upon hearing of Qaddafi's death on a television interview and pumped her fist: "We came, we saw, he died."[15]

President Obama subsequently said he felt that Libya had been the worst mistake of his presidency and that he and the Europeans should have invested more in trying to stabilize the country after Qaddafi's fall. Yet this would have required sending in military forces on the ground to try to keep the various armed militias apart, thereby exposing U.S. soldiers to attacks for no overriding national interest. The American public would have opposed this, especially given the U.S. commitments in Iraq and Afghanistan. With no support for any meaningful commitment to stabilize Libya, the United States never should have intervened in the first place.

How can one sum up the Libyan debacle? Prussian general and military theorist Carl von Clausewitz reportedly said, "A short jump is certainly easier than a long one: but no one wanting to get across a wide ditch would begin by jumping half-way." Or, as Gates later said in his criticism of the intervention, "In the use of military force, the words of Yoda from Star Wars apply: 'Do. Or do not. There is no try.'" Obama and other Western leaders only tried. Most of his senior advisers believed that they never should have tried.[16]

Certain foreign policy decisions are so clearly etched in history that they live on long afterward as examples of what to do or not to do in statecraft. John F. Kennedy's thoughtful deliberations during the Cuban missile crisis exemplify a successful approach to a crisis; Obama's red-line ultimatum in 2013 shows a leader who was given to making empty threats.

With the outbreak of political unrest in Syria in the spring of 2011, Obama released a statement calling on President Bashar al-Assad to step aside in August 2011. At the time, and in retrospect, a reasonable case could have been made either for or against military aerial intervention to attempt to overthrow Assad. U.S. aerial attacks against Syria's relatively weak military forces, such as those that took place in Libya, might have forced Assad to flee if they had occurred before Iranian and Hezbollah intervention in 2013. The fall of Assad would have been a huge blow to the Iran-Syria-Lebanon Hezbollah alliance. A chastened Iran might have been more cautious in its foreign policies and nuclear program.

In contrast, if Assad fell, no one could be certain what kind of Sunni ruler would emerge. It might have been a Sunni strongman opposed to Iranian influence, but it could also have been a religious ideologue. At least the secular Assad family generally avoided attacking Western targets (as opposed to Israeli ones).

In any case, in the wake of the Libyan imbroglio, Obama never considered seriously military intervention to overthrow Assad. During meetings with senior advisers on Syria Obama "often appeared impatient or disengaged while listening to the debate, sometimes scrolling through messages on his BlackBerry or slouching and chewing gum," according to participants.[17]

However, the Syrian government's use of chemical weapons was something that Obama felt he could not ignore, as Western intelligence obtained evidence of small-scale chemical weapons use beginning in the spring of 2012. The weapons were effective for creating terror, including clearing urban areas of opposition fighters and driving Sunni civilians from their homes, which would often be given to Assad's fellow Alawites.[18]

On August 20, 2012, Obama, to the surprise of his aides, made his first commitment to use military force for chemical weapons use: "We have been very clear to the Assad regime, but also to other players on the ground, that the red line for us is if we start seeing a whole bunch of chemical weapons moving around or being utilized. That would change my calculus. That would change my equation."[19]

Later, Secretary of Defense Panetta told journalist Jeffrey Goldberg that he did not know the statement would be made. Goldberg was also told that Vice President Biden repeatedly warned Obama against drawing a red line because he would have to enforce it at some point. However, Obama ignored Biden's advice and reiterated a statement in December 2012 that clearly implied the use of military force in response to any use of chemical weapons by Assad. Obama hoped the threat would deter the Syrian president from using them and from transferring the weapons to Lebanese Hezbollah.[20]

The chemical weapons issue came to a head when Syrian forces inflicted a large-scale chemical weapons attack on the Damascus suburb of Ghouta, killing about 1,500 civilians on August 21, 2013. In response, the United States, Britain, and France decided to resort to cruise-missile attacks between August 30 and September 2, dates that fell after the departure of UN chemical weapons inspectors but before the planned G20 summit on September 5. The French, who were the most supportive of the use of armed force, argued against bringing the issue before the Security Council, where Russia would obstruct or delay action. Militarily, everything quickly fell into place. The French and the British were integral parts of the U.S. planning process. An adviser to French defense minister Jean-Yves Le Drian would later say, "We had planned everything together, the Americans had opened all their books to us. For the first time, it was just the two of us in the bedroom."[21]

However, on August 29 Prime Minister Cameron lost a vote in Parliament authorizing British military involvement. Unlike the American and French presidents, a British prime minister was normally obligated to gain the approval of Parliament. The British vote, which reflected the disenchantment with the wars in Afghanistan, Iraq, and Libya, unnerved Obama, whose heart was never in his military initiative in the first place. He therefore informed his advisers that he would seek congressional approval for a strike, a surprising decision since Cameron had just lost his vote in Parliament. Obama's senior advisers were taken aback. Secretary of State Kerry reportedly told a friend, "I just got fucked over." Vice President Biden argued that "big nations don't bluff." However, Obama had made up his mind.[22]

Obama began to back out of his commitment by telling French president François Hollande on August 31 in a telephone conversation that he wanted to get congressional approval for an attack, which would take about fifteen days because they were in recess. Obama told Hollande that the British vote and the impossibility of reaching a consensus at the UN Security Council had changed his perspective.

Hollande, who was reportedly stunned by the conversation, again pointed out the perishable nature of the intelligence. French and U.S. naval vessels were within minutes of launching cruise-missile strikes when the orders came to stand down; French refueling aircraft, which had taken off from aircraft carriers, were recalled.

Obama continued to stake his reputation on a military commitment that he was deeply ambivalent about enforcing. Despite the stand-down, he announced in the Rose Garden that "the United States should take military action against Syrian regime targets" in order to support the taboo on the use of chemical weapons, reduce the risk of their acquisition by terrorists, and promote broader weapons of mass destruction objectives.[23] However, in early September, Obama learned that he would probably lose a vote for congressional authorization.

The confrontation entered its final phase with Secretary of State Kerry's sarcastic answer to a question at a press conference on September 9 about whether Assad could do anything to avoid an attack: "Sure. He could turn over every single bit of his chemical weapons to the international community in the next week. Turn it over, all of it, without delay, and allow a full and total accounting for that. But he isn't about to do it and it can't be done, obviously."[24] Yet, at the G20 meeting President Putin reportedly proposed just such a bargain the same day to Obama, perhaps not realizing that an attack was now highly unlikely. With little hope of gaining congressional approval for military action, the administration embraced the proposal.

Syria, in coordination with Russia, agreed to turn over its chemical weapons for destruction outside the country by international authorities over a period of several years. However, few believed that it would turn over all of the weapons; most expected surrender of only the less effective ones. Moreover, by requesting several years to turn over the chemical weapons, he reduced the incentives for Western adversaries to use military force or even to provide military assistance to the Syrian opposition since they now had a stake in his survival. It was a no-lose bargain for Assad, who would keep some of his chemical weapons clandestinely and replenish his supply with more advanced weapons. For Obama, it made retreat somewhat less embarrassing because he could claim that he had achieved the elimination of Assad's chemical weapons stockpile.[25] Assad's subsequent use of chemical weapons would prove the contrary.[26]

Senior U.S. officials in Obama's administration, including defense secretaries Gates, Panetta, Hagel, and Carter and secretaries of state Clinton and Kerry, subsequently criticized Obama's red-line incident. They made the obvious point: once Obama had staked his reputation on strikes, he should have followed through. If not, world leaders would take him less seriously.

Obama subsequently defended his decision by mocking the foreign policy establishment's so-called playbook:

> "Where am I controversial? When it comes to the use of military power," he said. "That is the source of the controversy. There's a playbook in Washington that presidents are supposed to follow. It's a playbook that comes out of the foreign-policy establishment. And the playbook prescribes responses to different events, and these responses tend to be militarized responses. Where America is directly threatened, the playbook works. But the playbook can also be a trap that can lead to bad decisions. In the midst of an international challenge like Syria, you get judged harshly if you don't follow the playbook, even if there are good reasons why it does not apply."[27]

Yet if Obama believed that the United States should not resort to military force unless it was directly threatened, why did he use it in Libya? And why had he shown such deep ambivalence rather than determination about using military force in response to what he said publicly was a major foreign policy interest, Syria's use of chemical weapons?

Obama's last secretary of defense, Ashton Carter, placed Obama's views about military power and diplomacy in perspective:

> Obama did sometimes exhibit a bit of overconfidence, even arrogance that can come from being both very smart and comparatively young. As an example, I'd point to his publicly expressed disdain for what he called "the Washington playbook"—the supposed set of unwritten guidelines for U.S. foreign policy dictated by "the establishment" and often parroted by mainstream pundits in the media and elsewhere. Obama would sometimes even appear to take mischievous pleasure in ignoring the playbook

and choosing an unconventional policy path—as if tweaking the playbook and the expectations of the establishment is a worthwhile goal in itself. He did this in 2013 when he decided not to enforce the red line.[28]

The French government was understandably furious at being abandoned by Obama at the last moment, and Foreign Minister Laurent Fabius believed that the red-line incident contributed to the Russian decision to invade Crimea and eastern Ukraine in 2014. Perhaps it also convinced Iran that it could drive a harder bargain in the negotiations over the 2015 nuclear deal and strengthened President Putin's conviction that he could brazenly interfere in the 2016 U.S. presidential election without any serious penalties.

We can never know the precise impact of this political retreat, but it did reinforce an impression, which existed already, that adversaries could oppose President Obama without paying a price. Perhaps King Abdullah of Jordan said it best: "I think I believe more in American power than President Obama does."[29]

Conclusion

Our studies of presidential foreign policy have illustrated some of the principles and recurring patterns of effective statecraft. These include the need to understand the complexity of issues, including the motivations and capabilities of other parties and the stakes for one's own country and its public opinion. Prudent leaders then examine the various policy options, including their pros and cons. Leaders and their advisers must also draw relevant lessons from the past, including from their own mistakes, adapt to changing circumstances in the present, and anticipate future developments. Finally, as noted, determination does not guarantee success, but its absence will result in failure.

These historical cases demonstrate that many of America's leading presidents had a deep understanding of complex situations. Washington and Hamilton understood the motivations and goals of the European powers. They worked with France during the American Revolution but did not encourage it to return to Canada and remained neutral during the 1790s wars of the French Revolution. Lincoln quickly mastered the nuances of European diplomacy. The two Roosevelts knew Europe and its languages from travel. They also understood the motivations of the European and Asian powers. Nixon, unlike nearly all other observers, anticipated that the Middle East was heading toward war in 1973 and foresaw its likely evolution; Secretary of State Kissinger navigated skillfully among the region's powers during the war and subsequent negotiations. President George H. W. Bush quickly realized that economic sanctions would not force Iraqi president Saddam Hussein out of Kuwait; he understood the policy implications of the oil market better than his senior advisers did.

Our historical cases also show that the presidents we consider successful were generally prudent in their policy choices. Washington made a point of asking his generals and civilian advisers for their advice about all key decisions, and he supported the unpopular Jay Treaty to avoid being dragged into a war with England. Lincoln wisely accepted the advice of Secretary of State Seward to postpone the Emancipation Proclamation until the North had achieved some military success, but rejected Secretary of the Navy Welles's counsel to challenge Britain's maritime policies at the risk of hostilities. As a mediator, Theodore Roosevelt helped to cajole Kaiser Wilhelm into backing down in Morocco in 1905. He also prodded Russian and Japanese officials into ending their war, for which he was awarded the Nobel prize. Franklin Roosevelt used guile and obfuscation to assist Britain and France against Germany without provoking damaging objections from Congress and public opinion. These presidents were all deliberative in their decision-making, examining policy options carefully.

Yet their prudence did not preclude bold choices. Lincoln fired a succession of generals until he found Grant. Franklin Roosevelt supported Churchill's decision to bomb the French fleet in 1940 to prevent it from falling under German control. Nixon approved placing U.S. military force on a high military alert status in 1973 to deter Soviet military intervention in the Arab-Israeli War. George H. W. Bush mobilized much of the U.S. military to expel Iraq from Kuwait in 1991.

Several presidents displayed the ability to learn, adapt and anticipate. Washington learned from his observations about European diplomacy and readings on military history. He also adapted his military strategy, however reluctantly, after military setbacks by the professional British Army. After the Russo-Japanese War, Theodore Roosevelt realized that Tokyo was the premier power in the Pacific and subsequently focused U.S. policy on containing a rising Japan. Franklin Roosevelt, Nixon, and George H. W. Bush learned from their service as vice presidents. Nixon and Kissinger anticipated that a rough stalemate in the 1973 Arab-Israeli War would make possible fruitful negotiations and therefore insisted that Israel not force the Egyptian Third Army to surrender. Bush anticipated that economic sanctions would not force Iraqi leader Saddam Hussein to withdraw from Kuwait and therefore pursued the military option.

Did any worldview unite these historic figures? Washington and Hamilton were comfortable with the traditional balance-of-power European approach to foreign policy, whereby concrete national interests were the highest priority. While they believed that the United States represented a noble experiment in self-government, unlike anything in Europe, they also felt America's foreign policy had to be conducted largely in the way of the European states. As noted, the word most often used in Washington's farewell address is *interest*, not freedom, liberty, or ideals. As Hamilton's biographer put it, "Unlike Jefferson, Hamilton never saw the creation of America as a magical leap across a chasm to an entirely new landscape, and he always thought the New World had much to learn from the Old."[1] Washington shared this view.

Lincoln, who was largely self-educated and not familiar with European writings about international relations, did not subscribe explicitly to any particular political philosophy. However, in the first major speech of his career, at the Young Men's Lyceum of Springfield in 1838, he called on Americans to rely on "reason—cold, calculating, unimpassioned reason," and spoke highly of President Washington.[2] As president, he leaned to the side of caution in diplomacy and of relentlessness in war.

Theodore Roosevelt and Henry Kissinger explicitly considered themselves to be in the realist tradition. Roosevelt's most frequent concept in his writings on foreign and military affairs was power. He wrote admiringly about the foreign policies of Washington and Hamilton while criticizing Jefferson, Madison, and Wilson for their overly moralistic approach to international politics and their unwillingness to back U.S. foreign policy adequately with military force. Kissinger often stated that American foreign policy had been too moralistic, and he wrote his first book on the realist diplomacy of the Congress of Vienna, with its Byzantine world of constant maneuvering for advantage. Franklin Roosevelt never identified explicitly with one political philosophy, but his diplomacy of guile and periodic moral compromise toward Vichy France in North Africa seemed to reflect a realist approach in practice, though not in public declaration. Realism, then, as practiced by these leaders, reflected not a set of policy prescriptions but a sensibility guided by enlightened self-interest.

The Decline of Statecraft?

Let us turn, however, to more recent presidents. As mentioned, Carter was the first candidate to be elected president since the 1920s without any foreign policy experience. Carter, moreover, was the first American politician to gain his party's nomination through the primary system rather than through the traditional process whereby party leaders, including senators, representatives, governors, and mayors, chose their nominee at a party convention. The primary system, which had been gaining ground over the years, reflected broader social trends toward greater democratization, public participation, and self-expression, and less deference to authority and hierarchy in general.

The impact of the primary system on U.S. foreign policy has been negative. The average voter, who is generally less interested in foreign policy and less educated than party leaders, has tended to vote for candidates with little foreign policy experience and, in some cases, even little interest in international affairs. Finally, Carter and his successors were products of a United States whose increasingly troubled domestic political scene resulted in voters seeking outsiders to run against "the establishment," including its generally centrist foreign policies.

Our case study of President Barack Obama's mistaken intervention in Libya in 2011 and his clumsy handling of Syria's use of chemical weapons reveals a certain tendency of inexperienced Democratic presidents such as Obama, Carter, and Clinton to shy away from forceful but prudent international policies, in contrast with the more seasoned Nixon and George H. W. Bush. Conversely, an inexperienced Republican president, George W. Bush, resorted to armed force too quickly. An even less experienced Republican leader, President Donald Trump, sought out confrontation for its own sake, but usually with friendly countries in Europe and Asia over trade deficits and defense spending. Trump was less interested in the balance of power than the balance of payments; he was more comfortable dealing with dictators than with democratic leaders. Republican Party leaders, unlike primary voters, would never have made Donald Trump their candidate.

Trump also ushered in a strong strain of isolationism to the Republican Party that heretofore had been stronger in the Democratic

Party. With the pro-Trump movement of less-well-educated voters into the Republican Party, its centrist internationalist wing lost strength. Similarly, the decline of centrist southern Democrats pushed the Democratic Party toward its liberal wing, which is inclined to excessive caution in foreign and military policy. Thus, inexperienced leaders and political polarization, exacerbated by divisive social media, have resulted in an increasingly erratic foreign policy.

Are there any domestic reforms that could counter these trends toward less effective statecraft? While returning to the days when party leaders chose presidential candidates is unlikely, reformists could establish nominating rules that would encourage bringing in party leaders, so-called superdelegates, toward the end of the electoral process to make a final choice. Conversely, one could adopt a system like that of the Conservative Party in Britain, whereby party leaders sift through the candidates and then call on all party members to vote for one of two candidates.

The most practical approach perhaps would be to promote the ranked-choice voting system, which is used in various forms in Maine, Alaska, and New York City, whereby voters rank candidates in order of their preference. This system tends to favor more loosely affiliated party members and independents and fewer ideological activists on the left and right. These long-term electoral reforms could help to walk the country back from the lure of the inexperienced outsider, polarization, and populism.[3]

A Return to Effective Statecraft

The international situation today presents three security challenges that call for effective statecraft: unfriendly great powers, hostile mid-sized powers armed with nuclear and biological weapons, and radical, violent terrorist groups. It will be important to keep these challenges under control or it will be more difficult to focus on new and vital non-security problems, such as climate change and out-of-control migration.

Both China and Russia have closed the military gap with the United States by the diffusion of technology, much of it from a readily available commercial sector. The days of completely self-contained and secretive military research are likely gone forever. Specifically, the development of mass sensors has enabled China and Russia to close the gap in precision-guided weapons that the United States began developing in the 1970s and used so effectively during the 1990s Gulf War. The proliferation of low-cost commercial sensors, including those on inexpensive satellites, has increased the ability of Russia and China to detect threats at longer distances. As one defense authority has said, "The world [is] becoming one giant sensor. . . . Stealth technology is living on borrowed time."[4] Moreover, both China and Russia have demonstrated impressive expertise in cyber operations. The United States is strong in this area, but it is also more vulnerable than Beijing and Moscow, given its greater connectivity.

Some have argued that the United States has the option of blockading oil imports in response to Chinese aggression; China imports about two-thirds of its oil consumption, of which about 85 percent arrives by sea. There are a number of problems with this scenario, however. First, a U.S. naval blockade would require the cooperation of the states bordering the Strait of Malacca—notably Indonesia, Malaysia, and Singapore, including access to their airfields—and perhaps of Saudi Arabia. Second, a recent study estimates that the United States would be able to inspect only about 25 percent of the merchant ships using the Southeast Asian straits; querying a higher proportion would not be feasible if there were competing demands to deploy U.S. naval ships to the South China Sea or Taiwan. Third, while a blockade of China would damage its economy, it would also wreak havoc on the international economy, given the importance of trade with China. China could also resort to rationing and to using its oil stockpile.[5] In short, the United States should not repeat Jefferson's mistake of overestimating its ability to apply economic coercion.

It is true that China's population will probably begin to contract in coming decades, whereas the U.S. population, despite a low birth rate, may continue to grow modestly because of immigration. However, America's current economic and military advantages will probably continue to erode, given that many of the Chinese living in small towns and the countryside will migrate to more productive urban areas. China, with its huge population, therefore probably still has a larger potential for economic growth than does the United States.

Prudence in Defense and Diplomacy

We have reviewed several occasions on which U.S. presidents failed because they did not provide adequate means, be they material or psychological, to support their goals. Jefferson and Madison cut the U.S. defense budget just as they adopted a more assertive policy toward English harassment of U.S. shipping. They also failed to allocate their defense spending optimally, as Theodore Roosevelt pointed out in his highly regarded book *The Naval War of 1812*. Roosevelt argued that instead of funding coastal barges to defend American ports, Jefferson and Madison should have prioritized oceangoing frigates to challenge British harassment on the high seas.

Is there a current mismatch between ends and means in U.S. defense policy? Yes, insofar as the United States is adopting a more assertive stance toward a rising China without providing adequate defense resources to undergird the policy. The United States currently spends slightly over 3 percent of its gross domestic product on defense. In contrast, during the early Cold War period it spent about 10 percent on defense, and during the 1980s around 8 percent. During the height of the Iraqi and Afghan wars in the first decade of the 2000s, Washington spent about 6 percent on defense. It would do well to spend about 4 percent on defense to adapt to the diffusion of military power throughout the world.

As important as an adequate defense budget is, so is an understanding of how to use it. Defense experts agree that the U.S. defense establishment relies too much on large, vulnerable surface ships, particularly aircraft carriers; sprawling military bases on land; and relatively large satellites in space. They are increasingly vulnerable to China, Russia, and others who have developed long-range precision missiles and modern sensors based on America's success in the first Gulf War. The surprisingly accurate Iranian attack on the huge Abqaiq oil complex in Saudi Arabia in 2019, which interrupted world oil supplies, reflected this trend. In fact, there will probably come a time when U.S. naval surface ships will be unable to operate safely in the Persian Gulf and close to China. Even non-state actors can threaten U.S. naval forces with new technologies; in 2006, for example, Hezbollah fired a Chinese surface-to-surface Silkworm missile provided by Iran that nearly sank the Israeli corvette *Hanit*.

Thus, the United States must adapt to this new environment by moving in the direction of smaller, more dispersed, and cheaper autonomous military systems, just as the U.S. commercial computer industry moved away from large mainframes to smaller devices. There is a consensus among defense intellectuals on this direction, but it will require determined leadership from the president and congressional leaders to overcome inertia, a perceived lack of urgency, and the vested interests of much of the armed services and Congress. It may require a president who is truly conversant with defense reform issues, such as Theodore Roosevelt.[6]

At the same time, the United States cannot succumb to erratic diplomacy toward its two most powerful rivals, Russia and China. U.S. diplomacy with Russia since the end of the Cold War is a good example of what not to do. Rather than overreaching in its quest to expand NATO, to avoid provoking Russia the United States could have sought a middle path by extending NATO membership to Poland, Hungary, and the Czech and Slovak Republics, but not to countries bordering Russia, notably the Baltic states, Ukraine, and Georgia. Ideally, these countries, like Finland during the Cold War, could have developed pluralistic democracies without being seen as a security threat by Moscow. Instead, an overly confident President George W. Bush pushed successfully for NATO membership for the Baltic states in 2004 and unsuccessfully for NATO membership for Ukraine and Georgia in 2008. This contributed to turning a somewhat unfriendly President Putin into a true adversary and resulted in the Russian invasion of Georgia in 2008.

The Obama administration then sided conspicuously with the anti-Russian political movement in 2014 in a highly polarized Ukraine while refusing lethal military equipment to Kiev when Moscow invaded parts of eastern Ukraine in the same year. This contradictory policy recalled Jefferson and Madison cutting the defense budget as they embarked on a more aggressive policy toward England. President Trump sent lethal military equipment to Ukraine but did not grant the permission to use it against Russian forces in eastern Ukraine. Otherwise, he conveyed to Moscow that his sole interest in Ukraine was to use it to cast aspersions on the business operations there of Joe Biden's son. Perhaps Putin would have invaded Ukraine under any circumstances, but U.S. diplomacy toward Moscow has been inconsistent.

With respect to China the United States must conduct a rivalry in Asia for the foreseeable future, and probably globally, without turning the contest into a pro-democracy crusade against the Chinese Communist Party. The United States will be able to pursue this rivalry with the knowledge that it has powerful allies in Asia and Europe and partners in much of the rest of the world where the widespread use of the English language helps to create influence.

China, for its part, seeks not war but rather deference from other Asian powers, as was the case in its imperial past. To achieve this, Beijing hopes gradually but inexorably to reduce the influence of the United States and its partners in East Asia, in part by intimidating Western partners such as Japan and Australia through military and commercial power and cultivating others such as South Korea and the Philippines. There are, however, some positive factors favoring the United States. The Chinese elite still sends many of its children to the West for their education, and a vast network of commercial ties between China and the United States and its partners tends to work to constrain Beijing.

The Challenge of Radical States and Terrorist Movements

The ongoing diffusion of military technology will probably continue to reduce America's traditional military advantages even over midsize powers. North Korea's nuclear inventory may rival that of France or Britain, and it has the capacity to develop intercontinental missiles that could hit the United Strikes. There is no serious preventive U.S. military option against the program because much of it is underground and dispersed and Pyongyang would retaliate against the citizens of Seoul in the event of a U.S. attack. Similarly, Iran could attempt to develop nuclear weapons with intercontinental missiles. The prospect of a nuclear North Korea or Iran raises some horrifying worst-case scenarios. Future leaders may not want to rule out the use of precise, low-yield nuclear weapons against countries on the verge of using nuclear arms from well-defended bunkers, or against terrorists on the verge of gaining possession of nuclear weapons in a collapsing state or forcing military officers to initiate their use.[7] As we have seen, statecraft sometimes calls for audacity, as epitomized by Churchill's order of an attack on the French fleet in July 1940.

However, the most serious military threat, principally from radical Islamist states and movements, may be biological warfare. The current revolution in bioengineering, the manipulation of an organism's genetic material, is making the production and use of biological weapons easier and more lethal. Already, a team of scientists at China's National Avian Influenza Reference Laboratory combined H5N1 avian flu with other kinds of influenza in the 2010s. International scientists condemned their experimentation because new forms of flu could have escaped the laboratory. While the Chinese team presumably had no malevolent goals, continuing advances in widely known bioengineering techniques could allow states, and perhaps even small terrorist organizations, to modify and release new forms of existing viruses to create pandemics that could dwarf the COVID-19 virus of the early 2020s.

The most dangerous scenario is for terrorists to reengineer existing viruses to create human-to-human transmissible versions. For example, avian flu is currently largely restricted to birds but has a lethality of 60 percent in the rare cases where it inflects humans. Ebola has been largely restricted to parts of Africa but has a lethality rate of about 50 percent. Moreover, a sophisticated terrorist group could try to modify a deadly virus to have a longer latency period, which would facilitate its undetected spread. The targeted country might not even know who the attacker was.[8]

WE HAVE SEEN that several of our most successful political leaders made difficult moral compromises for the greater good. Washington and Hamilton favored the idea of republican government, but in order to maintain American neutrality they opposed supporting the new French republic despite France's assistance during the American Revolution. Theodore Roosevelt acquiesced in the Japanese annexation of Korea, about which the United States could do nothing, in the hopes that Tokyo would balance Russia on the Asian mainland rather than expand into the Pacific. President Franklin Roosevelt did not recoil from the ferocity of the bombing of German and Japanese cities during the war. National Security Adviser Brzezinski urged President Carter to encourage the shah of Iran to crack down on the opposition to avoid revolutionary chaos. In short, effective statecraft sometimes calls for moral compromises.

A future U.S. president might be confronted with such decisions in response, for example, to mass deaths caused by biological attacks, and the correct choice would depend on the particular circumstances. President Obama issued an executive order banning the harsh interrogation techniques used during the first George W. Bush administration. If U.S. authorities held suspects involved in such attacks, idealists would argue that torture, like slavery, is always wrong. Realists would answer that that may be true, but, as Franklin Roosevelt said about his dealings with Vichy French officials, sometimes a lesser wrong is necessary to avoid a much greater wrong.[9] Whatever the security challenges that emerge in the coming years, future presidents can take lessons, and even inspiration, from America's most iconic leaders from the past.

NOTES

Notes to Introduction

1. Andrew Roberts, *Leadership in War* (New York: Viking, 2019), 221.
2. Ibid.

Chapter 1

1. For Churchill's views, see Henry Kissinger, *Diplomacy* (New York: Simon and Schuster, 1994), 632–33. Kissinger's book is an excellent survey of five centuries of European and American diplomacy and history. For views of Kennan and Lippmann, see ibid., 465–66. For more on Churchill's views, see Martin Gilbert, *Winston S. Churchill*, vol. 8, *Never Despair, 1945–1965* (Boston: Houghton Mifflin, 1988), 973–74.
2. Richard Neustadt and Ernest May, *Thinking in Time: The Uses of History for Decision Makers* (New York: Free Press, 1988).
3. Jennifer See, "A Prophet without Honor: Hans Morgenthau and the War in Vietnam, 1955–1965," *Pacific Historical Review* 70, no. 3 (August 2001): 419–48. For a biography of Morgenthau, see Christoph Frei, *Hans J. Morgenthau: An Intellectual Biography* (Baton Rouge: Louisiana State University Press, 2001).
4. Edmund Burke, "Letter to the Sheriffs of Bristol," in *The Works of Edmund Burke*, vol. 2 (London: George Bell and Sons, 1905), 28.
5. James McPherson, *Battle Cry of Freedom* (New York: Oxford University Press, 1988), 505.
6. Eliot Cohen, *Supreme Command* (New York: Free Press, 2002), 22. A brilliant study on civilian-military relations with chapters of the wartime leadership of Lincoln, Clemenceau, Churchill, and Ben-Gurion.
7. Colin Powell, *My American Journey* (New York: Random House, 1995), 485.
8. Walter Lippmann, *U.S. Foreign Policy: Shield of the Republic* (Boston: Atlantic Monthly Press, 1943). For a fine biography of America's most famous foreign policy journalist in the twentieth century, see Ronald Steel, *Walter*

Lippmann and the American Century (Boston: Little, Brown, 1980). Lippmann knew all the presidents from Theodore Roosevelt through Richard Nixon. He had the greatest respect (and personal liking) for Theodore Roosevelt.

9. Don Oberdorfer, "Kissinger Oversleeps on His Last Day," *Washington Post*, January 20, 1977.

10. Robert Dallek, *Franklin D. Roosevelt and American Foreign Policy, 1932–1945* (New York: Oxford University Press, 1995), 336.

11. McPherson, *Battle Cry of Freedom*, 271.

12. Duff Cooper, *Talleyrand* (New York: Grove Press, 1932), 177–78. Cooper was a parliamentary colleague and ally of Churchill during the 1930s. As a political realist, Cooper generally respected Talleyrand and disliked Thomas Jefferson, whose foreign policy he considered naïve and whose idealism he thought hypocritical because of slavery. Cooper is part of a laudable tradition of British political leaders who write books on the great figures in British history, including Churchill's study of the Duke of Marlborough. For those interested in a brilliant overview of European power politics, see Martin Wight, *Power Politics*, edited by Hedley Bull and Carsten Holbraad (London: Leister University Press, 1978).

13. Irving Janis, *Groupthink: Psychological Studies of Policy Decision and Fiascoes* (Boston: Houghton Mifflin, 1972).

14. For the Somalia debacle, see Walter Poole, *The Effort to Save Somalia* (Washington, DC: Joint History Office, Office of the Chairman of the Joint Chiefs of Staff, 2005). For the failure in Lebanon, see Benis Frank, *U.S. Marines in Lebanon 1982–1984* (Washington, DC: History and Museums Division Headquarters, U.S. Marine Corps, 1987).

15. Author's discussions with U.S. military officials, summer 2022.

16. For the debate within the Clinton administration, see Richard Clarke, *Against All Enemies: Inside America's War on Terror* (New York: Free Press, 2004), 181–204.

17. For the internal U.S. government debates, see Robert Gates, *Duty: Memoirs of a Secretary at War* (New York: Alfred Knopf, 2014), 335–86. It is an excellent account of the George W. Bush and Barack Obama foreign policy periods. For the best history about the U.S. involvement, see Carter Malkasian, *The American War in Afghanistan* (New York: Oxford University Press, 2021).

18. Hans Morgenthau, *Politics among Nations* (New York: McGraw-Hill, 1948). Perhaps the most famous book advocating a realist foreign policy. Morgenthau supported an assertive American foreign policy while recognizing the need for limits. As mentioned, he was an early critic of the Vietnam War. For an excellent discussion of foreign policy and morality, see Owen Harries, *Morality and Foreign Policy*, Occasional Paper 94 (November 19, 2004), Centre for Independent Studies, https://www.cis.org.au/publication/morality-and-foreign-policy/. Harries was the editor of *The National Interest*, a U.S. publication that tends toward the realist point of view.

19. Henry Kissinger, *White House Years* (Boston: Little, Brown, 1979), 622.

20. Cohen, *Supreme Command*, 166.

21. For a detailed look at this example of audacity, see Thomas Parker, "When Churchill Bombed France," *National Interest* 145 (September/October 2016): 77–84.

22. For Eisenhower's regrets about his policy choices over the Suez crisis, see Peter Rodman, *Presidential Command* (New York: Alfred A. Knopf, 2009), 27–28. A close associate of Kissinger, Rodman focuses on the relationships between post–World War II presidents and their State and Defense Departments. It is one of the finest books on post–World War II foreign policy up through the George W. Bush administration.

23. Dallek, *Franklin D. Roosevelt and American Foreign Policy,* 365.

24. For background on the U.S. involvement in Lebanon, see Rodman, *Presidential Command*, 170–73. See also (at CIA.gov) David Kennedy and Leslie Brunetta, *Lebanon and the Intelligence Community* (Washington, DC: Center for the Study of Intelligence, 1988). For background on Somalia, see Colin Powell, *My American Journey* (New York: Random House, 1995); Henry Kissinger, "Somalia Reservations," *Washington Post*, December 13, 1992. Powell, like most of the U.S. military, opposed the humanitarian intervention in Somalia.

25. For an interesting differing point of view in favor of democracy promotion, see Elliott Abrams, *Realism and Democracy* (New York: Cambridge University Press, 2017).

Chapter 2

1. For the Morris incident, see April 10, 2015, at *Boston 1775*, http://boston1775.blogspot.com/2015/04/did-gouverneur-morris-slap-washington.html. For Jefferson's quote, see Ron Chernow, *Alexander Hamilton* (New York: Penguin Books, 2005), 290. Chernow's book is the most comprehensive biography on Hamilton. Richard Brookhiser's *Alexander Hamilton, American* (New York: Free Press, 1999), is a shorter biography that is extremely incisive and well-written. Both books would appeal to the scholar, student, and general reader.

2. Joseph Ellis, *His Excellency George Washington* (New York: Vintage Books, 2004), 107. This biography covers Washington's reluctant shift away from conventional war and toward guerrilla war.

3. For Washington as war leader, see Ellis, *His Excellency George Washington*, 73–109; Richard Brookhiser, *Founding Father: Rediscovering George Washington* (New York: Free Press, 1996), 17–45; Russell Weigley, *The American Way of War* (Bloomington: Indiana University Press, 1973), 3–39; Thomas Fleming, "Escape from Brooklyn," *Quarterly Journal of Military History* 25 (Summer 2013): 28–37. Ellis and Brookhiser provide the best general biographies on Washington and are extremely readable and incisive; they would appeal to the scholar, student, and general reader.

4. Ellis, *His Excellency George Washington*, 123.

5. Eliot Cohen, *Conquered Into Liberty: Two Centuries of Battles Along the Great Warpath that Made the American War of War* (New York: Free Press, 2011), 249.

6. Chernow, *Alexander Hamilton*, 317–18.

7. "Conversation with a Committee of the United States House of Representatives," quoted from Jefferson's Memoranda of Consultations with the President, 11 Mar.–9 April 1792 (DLC: Jefferson Papers), *Founders Online*, National Archives, https://founders.archives.gov/documents/Washington/05 -10-02-0045.

8. To Thomas Jefferson from William Short, July 20, 1792, *Founders Online*, National Archives, https://founders.archives.gov/documents/Jefferson /01-24-02-0227; From Thomas Jefferson to William Short, January 3, 1793, *Founders Online*, National Archives, https://founders.archives.gov/documents /Jefferson/01-25-02-0016.

9. Chernow, *Alexander Hamilton*, 431–37; Joseph Ellis, *American Sphinx: the Character of Thomas Jefferson* (New York: Vintage Books, 1998), 129–30, 133–38, 149–51. For the best comparison of the outlooks of Hamilton and Jefferson, see Robert Tucker and David Hendrickson, *Empire of Liberty: The Statecraft of Thomas Jefferson* (New York: Oxford University Press, 1990), 33–47. The latter is considered the best work on Jefferson's foreign policy. Tucker and Hendrickson point out that while Jefferson made the Louisiana Purchase, he did so with an ambivalence about his use of executive power. Ellis's *American Sphinx* is a superb biography of Jefferson. Like his biography on Washington, it can appeal to the scholar, student, and general reader. For more on Hamilton's foreign policy views, see John Lamberton Harper, *American Machiavelli: Alexander Hamilton and the Origins of U.S. Foreign Policy* (Cambridge: Cambridge University Press, 2004).

10. Henry Essex Edgeworth de Firmont and Charles Sneyd Edgeworth, *Memoirs of the Abbe Edgeworth: Containing the Narrative of the Last Hours of Louis XVI* (London: Rowland Hunter, 1815).

11. Paul Schroeder, *The Transformation of European Politics, 1763–1848* (Oxford: Clarendon Press, 1994), 67–74, 157–58. Schroeder is one of the leading U.S. historians of nineteenth-century European foreign relations. He also wrote interestingly about the conceptual aspects of international relations for such publications as *International Security*. The author once asked Schroeder at a conference about Henry Kissinger's study on the Congress of Vienna. Schroeder replied that Kissinger had interesting things to say, but he did not elaborate. The author found that Kissinger's comments about the motives of the Congress's diplomats were interesting but speculative.

12. Pacificus, no. IV (July 10, 1793), *Founders Online*, National Archives, https://founders.archives.gov/documents/Hamilton/01-15-02-0066.

13. Thomas Jefferson to James Madison, July 7, 1793, *Founders Online*, National Archives, https://founders.archives.gov/documents/Jefferson/01-26 -02-0391.

14. For the neutrality debate, see Tucker and Hendrickson, *Empire of Liberty*, 48–63; Bradford Perkins, *The Creation of the American Empire, 1776– 1865* (Cambridge: Cambridge University Press, 1993), 87–95; Joseph Ellis, *Founding Brothers* (New York: Vintage Books, 2000), 134–36; Brookhiser, *Alexander Hamilton, American*, 92–93; Chernow, *Alexander Hamilton*, 435–47.

15. Tucker and Hendrickson, *Empire of Liberty*, 78.

16. Chernow, *Alexander Hamilton*, 458–67; Denver Brunsman, "Subjects vs. Citizens," *Journal of the Early Republic* 30 (Winter 2010): 571–73.

17. Alexander Hamilton to George Washington, April 14, 1794, *Founders Online*, National Archives, https://founders.archives.gov/documents/Hamilton/01-16-02-0208-0002.

18. Alexander Hamilton, *The Defence* No. V, August 5, 1795, *Founders Online*, National Archives, https://founders.archives.gov/documents/Hamilton/01-19-02-0008; Brookhiser, *Alexander Hamilton, American*, 124.

19. Brookhiser, *Alexander Hamilton, American*, 124.

20. Ellis, *American Sphinx*, 186–94; Brookhiser, *Alexander Hamilton, American*, 123–26.

21. Ellis, *His Excellency George Washington*, 226–32. For background on the Jay Treaty, see Tucker and Hendrickson, *Empire of Liberty*, 64–73; Brookhiser, *Alexander Hamilton, American*, 95–100; Chernow, *Alexander Hamilton*, 485–503.

22. For a brilliant analysis of the Farewell Address and its place in the British foreign policy realist tradition of the period, see Felix Gilbert, *To the Farewell Address* (Princeton, NJ: Princeton University Press, 1961). Gilbert, like Hans Morgenthau and Henry Kissinger, fled Germany in the 1930s. Ellis, *Founding Brothers*, 153.

23. Tucker and Hendrickson cover the entire Jefferson period in *Empire of Liberty*.

24. Michael Beschloss, *Presidents of War* (New York: Crown, 2018), 7–36. Beschloss praises Jefferson for keeping the United States out of war, unlike Madison, but does not note that Jefferson's unsuccessful economic sanctions contributed to eventual military hostilities.

25. Beschloss, *Presidents of War*, 70.

26. Chernow, *Alexander Hamilton*, 317–18.

27. For Jefferson's controversial conduct as governor of Virginia, see Ellis, *American Sphinx*, 77.

28. For the growth of the middle-class antagonism toward the aristocracy's control of foreign policy, see Michael Howard, *War and the Liberal Conscience* (New Brunswick, NJ: Rutgers University Press, 1989), 13–30. The book is a brilliant analysis of the changing Western attitudes toward war from the Renaissance to the modern era.

29. Thomas Jefferson to James Madison, 28 August 1789, *Founders Online*, National Archives, https://founders.archives.gov/documents/Jefferson/01-15-02-0354.

30. For Lincoln's admiration of Washington, see Fred Kaplan, *Lincoln: The Biography of a Writer* (New York: HarperCollins, 2008), 77–79.

Chapter 3

1. Dean Mahin, *One War at a Time: The International Dimensions of the American Civil War* (Washington, DC: Brassey's, 2000), 1.

2. Ibid., 5.

3. For Lincoln's extensive involvement in foreign policy, see Mahin, *One War at a Time*, 1–14. For Seward's role, see Norman Ferris, *Desperate Diplomacy: William Seward's Foreign Policy, 1861* (Knoxville: University of Tennessee Press, 1976).

4. Mahin, *One War at a Time*, 9.

5. Ibid., 44–57; James McPherson, *Battle Cry of Freedom* (Oxford: Oxford University Press, 1988), 387–89.

6. Kenneth Bourne, *Britain and the Balance of Power in North America, 1815–1908* (Berkeley: University of California Press, 1967), 245.

7. Bourne, *Britain and Balance of Power*, 244–45. For British diplomacy and military plans for war during the *Trent* affair, see ibid., 206–47. For the impact of slavery on U.S., British, and French policy, see Howard Jones, *Abraham Lincoln and a New Birth of Freedom: The Union and Slavery in the Diplomacy of the Civil War* (Lincoln: University of Nebraska Press, 1999). For an in-depth analysis on the role of the prize cases in Civil War diplomacy, see Stuart Bernath, *Squall across the Atlantic* (Berkeley: University of California Press, 1970).

8. Mahin, *One War at a Time*, 75–77.

9. Ibid., 80.

10. Ibid., 58–82; McPherson, *Battle Cry of Freedom*, 369–91.

11. McPherson, *Battle Cry of Freedom*, 505.

12. Mahin, *One War at a Time*, 138.

13. Ibid., 131.

14. Ibid., 139–41. For the diplomacy of 1862, including the impact of the cotton trade, see also McPherson, *Battle Cry of Freedom*, 546–67.

15. Mahin, *One War at a Time*, 187.

16. Ibid., 141.

17. For Lincoln's steps to conciliate Britain, see ibid., 185–96.

18. For penetrating accounts of Lincoln as war commander, see Eliot Cohen, *Supreme Command: Soldiers, Statesmen, and Leadership in Wartime* (New York: Free Press, 2002), and James McPherson, *Tried by War: Abraham Lincoln as Commander in Chief* (London: Penguin, 2008).

Chapter 4

1. Edmund Morris, *Theodore Rex* (New York: Modern Library, 2002), 323–38. Morris covers the Perdicaris affair. Secretary of State John Hay coined the dramatic phrase. In fact, Roosevelt and Hay acted quite cautiously during the incident despite the macho statement.

2. Theodore Roosevelt, "National Duties," in *Theodore Roosevelt: Letters and Speeches*, edited by Louis Auchincloss (New York: Library of America, 2004), 772.

3. Howard Beale, *Theodore Roosevelt and the Rise of America to World Power* (New York: Collier, 1967), 49.

4. Ibid. The confrontation ended with the two countries partitioning the islands.

5. Theodore Roosevelt to William Cowles, December 22, 1895, in Theodore Roosevelt, *The Selected Letters of Theodore Roosevelt*, edited by H. W. Brands (New York: Cooper Square, 2001), 112.

6. Beale, *Theodore Roosevelt*, 61.

7. John Davis Long, *America of Yesterday: As Reflected in the Journal of John Davis Long*, edited by Lawrence Shaw Mayo (Boston: Atlantic Monthly, 1923), 168–69, 186, 188 (entries for April 25 and May 5, 1898).

8. Roosevelt, *Selected Letters*, 132.

9. Ibid., 153–54.

10. William Michael Morgan, *Pacific Gibraltar: U.S.-Japanese Rivalry over the Annexation of Hawaii, 1885–1898* (Annapolis, MD: Naval Institute, 2011).

11. William Armstrong, *Major McKinley: William McKinley and the Civil War* (Kent, OH: Kent State University Press, 2000).

12. Kenneth Bourne, *Britain and the Balance of Power in North America 1815–1908* (Berkeley: University of California Press, 1967) 346–51; Beale, *Theodore Roosevelt*, 85–158 passim.

13. Beale, *Theodore Roosevelt*, 96.

14. Theodore Roosevelt, *Letters from Theodore Roosevelt to Anna Roosevelt Cowles, 1870–1918* (New York: Charles Scribner's Sons, 1924), 234.

15. Beale, *Theodore Roosevelt*, 85–158.

16. Roosevelt, *Selected Letters*, 142.

17. Ibid., 143, 170.

18. Ibid., 143, 230–31.

19. Beale, *Theodore Roosevelt*, 340–69 passim.

20. Raymond Esthus, *Theodore Roosevelt and the International Rivalries* (Claremont, CA: Regina Books, 1982) 47, 59.

21. Ibid., 77–78.

22. Ibid., 105.

23. See ibid., 66–111 passim, on the crisis over Morocco.

24. Beale, *Theodore Roosevelt*, 226–27.

25. Ibid., 230–31.

26. Ibid., 224–89 passim.

27. Roosevelt, *Selected Letters*, 354.

28. Esthus, *Theodore Roosevelt*, 31.

29. Beale, *Theodore Roosevelt*, 235; Roosevelt, *Selected Letters*, 361–65.

30. This last point would resemble Secretary of State Henry Kissinger's support of Israel during the 1973 Arab-Israeli War with an eye toward seeking Israeli compromises during the postwar negotiations, which will be discussed later in this book.

31. Beale, *Theodore Roosevelt*, 248–51.

32. Esthus, *Theodore Roosevelt*, 34.

33. Tyler Dennett, *Roosevelt and the Russo-Japanese War* (New York: Peter Smith, 1925), 320. On Roosevelt and the Russo-Japanese War, see Beale, *Theodore Roosevelt*, 234–73 passim; Esthus, *Theodore Roosevelt*, 25–37; Roosevelt, *Selected Letters*, 380–84, 437, 463. For an interesting overview of Roosevelt's policy in Asia, see Michael J. Green, *By More than Providence: Grand Strategy*

and American Power in the Asia Pacific since 1783 (New York: Columbia University Press, 2017), 78–113.

34. Esthus, *Theodore Roosevelt,* 136–50.

35. Theodore Roosevelt, *The Works of Theodore Roosevelt,* vol. 23 (New York: Charles Scribner's Sons, 1926), 323.

36. On the Panama Canal, see Beale, *Theodore Roosevelt,* 101–108; on Cuba, see Edmund Morris, *Theodore Rex* (New York: Modern Library, 2002), 101–106, 456–64; on the Dominican Republic, see Morris, *Theodore Rex,* 319; on the Hague Conference, see Beale, *Theodore Roosevelt,* 293.

37. For the quote on the Dominican issue, see Joseph Bucklin Bishop, *Theodore Roosevelt and His Time, Shown in His Own Letters,* vol. 1 (New York: Charles Scribner's Sons, 1920), 431. For the Latin American debt issue, see Beale, *Theodore Roosevelt,* 293.

38. Roosevelt, *Selected Letters,* 577.

39. John Milton Cooper Jr. *The Warrior and the Priest: Woodrow Wilson and Theodore Roosevelt* (Cambridge, MA: Belknap Press, 1996), 285.

40. Ibid., 310.

41. Roosevelt, *Selected Letters,* 614.

42. William Widenor, *Henry Cabot Lodge and the Search for an American Foreign Policy* (Berkeley: University of California Press, 1980), 292, 302.

43. Woodrow Wilson, Address to Naturalized Citizens at Convention Hall, Philadelphia, May 10, 1915, The American Presidency Project, https://www .presidency.ucsb.edu/documents/address-naturalized-citizens-convention-hall -philadelphia.

44. Cooper, *The Warrior and the Priest,* 310–11.

45. Widenor, *Henry Cabot Lodge,* 274.

46. Cooper, *The Warrior and the Priest,* 112.

Chapter 5

1. Robert Dallek, *Franklin Roosevelt and American Foreign Policy, 1932–1945* (Oxford: Oxford University Press, 1995), 365. Dallek's book is the most complete study of Roosevelt's foreign policy. Dallek's periodic criticism of Roosevelt and his bold use of executive power sometimes has a dovish tone, perhaps reflecting the anti-military attitude of the 1970s Vietnam War decade, when the book was originally published.

2. Henry Kissinger, *Diplomacy* (New York: Simon & Schuster, 1994), 380; Dallek, *Franklin Roosevelt,* 80–81.

3. Dallek, *Franklin Roosevelt,* 75–76, 88–90.

4. Ibid., 110–21.

5. Ibid., 129.

6. *Congressional Record,* volume 90, part 3, *March 22, 1944, to May 11, 1944* (Washington, DC: Government Printing Office, 1944), April 21, 3620.

7. Ibid., 152; Kissinger, *Diplomacy,* 379.

8. Dallek, *Franklin Roosevelt,* 153–56.

9. Ibid., 164.

10. Ibid.

11. Kissinger, *Diplomacy*, 380–82; Dallek, *Franklin Roosevelt*, 161–66; Franklin D. Roosevelt, *Complete Presidential Press Conferences of Franklin Delano Roosevelt*, vol. 12, 1938 (New York: Da Capo, 1972).

12. Dallek, *Franklin Roosevelt*, 174.

13. Thomas G. Paterson, J. Garry Clifford, Robert Brigham, Michael Donoghue, Kenneth J. Hagan, Deborah Kisatsky, and Shane J. Maddock, *American Foreign Relations: A History*, vol. 2, *Since 1895*, 7th ed. (Boston: Wadsworth, 2010), 112–15; Dallek, *Franklin Roosevelt*, 174–75.

14. Dallek, *Franklin Roosevelt*, 172.

15. Dallek, *Franklin Roosevelt*, 173–74.

16. Ibid., 181.

17. Ibid., 181–91.

18. Ibid., 196–97.

19. Ibid., 199.

20. Ibid., 200–204.

21. Ibid., 213.

22. Ibid., 243.

23. Eric Seal, "Churchill at War," *The Times* (London, England), January 4, 1969.

24. Winston Churchill, *The Collected Works* (n.l.: DigiCat, 2022), chapter 11, n.p.

25. For this unparalleled example of audacity in war, see the following articles: Thomas Parker, "When Churchill Bombed France," *National Interest* 145 (September/October 2016), 77; Douglas Porch, *The Path to Victory: The Mediterranean Theatre in World War II* (Old Saybrook, CT: Konecky & Konecky, 2004), 63–69; Arthur Marder, *From the Dardanelles to Oran: Studies in the Royal Navy in War and Peace, 1915–1940* (London: Oxford University Press, 1974); Richard Lamb, *Churchill as War Leader* (New York: Carroll and Graf, 1991). Marder's is the most detailed account in English on Churchill's attack. Churchill considered this to be his most difficult decision during the war. Most English-speaking commentators believe that Churchill probably made the right decision, given the dangers of the fleet falling under German control. For De Gaulle's reported expression of understanding of the decision, at least privately, see Henry Kissinger, *Leadership* (New York: Penguin Press, 2022), 65.

26. Eric Larrabee, *Commander in Chief: Franklin Delano Roosevelt, His Lieutenants, and Their War* (New York: Simon and Schuster, 1988), 51.

27. For the scope of the cooperation, see Robert Sherwood, *Roosevelt and Hopkins: An Intimate History* (New York: Enigma Books, 2001), 265–66.

28. Ibid., 257; Dallek, *Franklin Roosevelt*, 248–61.

29. Mark Stoler, *Allies in War: Britain and America against the Axis Powers* (London: Hodder Arnold, 2007), 26; Dallek, *Franklin Roosevelt*, 261–62; Sherwood, *Roosevelt and Hopkins*, 283; Franklin D. Roosevelt and Winston Churchill, *Roosevelt and Churchill: Their Secret Wartime Correspondence*,

edited by Francis L. Loewenheim, Harold D. Langley, and Manfred Jonas (New York: Da Capo, 1975), 137.

30. Larrabee, *Commander in Chief*, 51.

31. Ibid., 55; Roosevelt and Churchill, *Secret Wartime Correspondence*, 42.

32. Dallek, *Franklin Roosevelt*, 265–68.

33. Ibid., 276.

34. Ibid., 282.

35. Ibid., 281–87.

36. Ibid., 287–89.

37. Ibid., 285.

38. Ibid., 288.

Chapter 6

1. Robert J. Donovan, *Tumultuous Years: The Presidency of Harry Truman, 1949–1953* (New York: W.W. Norton, 1982), 91–92.

2. Henry Kissinger, *Diplomacy* (New York: Simon & Schuster, 1994), 474–75. Soviet documents declassified during the 1990s under President Boris Yeltsin show that Soviet authorities never seriously considered launching a premeditated invasion of Western Europe during the Cold War. This does not rule out consideration of a preemptive attack as a result of their misunderstanding of Western intentions.

3. William Stueck, *The Korean War: An International History* (Princeton, NJ: Princeton University Press, 1997), 25; George Kennan, *Memoirs, 1925–1950* (Boston: Little, Brown, 1967), 170–72.

4. Harry Truman, *Years of Trial and Hope*, vol. 2, *1943–1952* (Garden City, NY: Doubleday, 1956), 324–30.

5. Stueck, *Korean War*, 376.

6. Robert Beisner, *Dean Acheson: A Life in the Cold War* (Oxford: Oxford University Press, 2009), 325–26; Alexander George and Richard Smoke, *Deterrence in American Foreign Policy: Theory and Practice* (New York: Colombia University Press, 1974), 143.

7. Donovan, *Tumultuous Years*, 95.

8. Dean Acheson, *Present at the Creation* (New York: W.W. Norton, 1969), 355–58.

9. Beisner, *Dean Acheson*, 326–27.

10. Ibid., 326–27.

11. Clayton Laurie, "The Korean War and the Central Intelligence Agency," in *Baptism by Fire: CIA Analysis of the Korean War* (Washington, DC: Center for the Study of Intelligence, 2010), https://www.cia.gov/readingroom/docs/2010-05-01.pdf.

12. Truman, *Years of Trial and Hope*, 331–48.

13. Donovan, *Tumultuous Years*, 212.

14. Eliot Cohen and John Gooch, *Military Misfortunes: The Anatomy of Failure in War* (New York: Vintage, 1991), 165–66.

15. John Lewis Gaddis, *George Kennan: An American Life* (New York: Penguin, 2011), 399–400.

16. Donovan, *Tumultuous Years*, 268–73.

17. Ibid.

18. Cohen and Gooch, *Military Misfortunes*, 165–75; Kissinger, *Diplomacy*, 481; U.S. State Department, *Foreign Relations of the United States 7* (1950): 936.

19. While U.S. and South Korean forces were the most important component in the international military coalition, European countries—especially the United Kingdom and France—and Turkey played very useful roles. Other countries, including the Philippines and India, made modest contributions.

20. Stueck, *Korean War*, 134–35; Gaddis, *George Kennan*, 413.

21. Kennan, *Memoirs*, 488; Kissinger, *Diplomacy*, 480, 488.

22. For a detailed account of Chinese strategy, see Donggil Kim, "China's Intervention in the Korean War Revisited," *Diplomatic History* 40, no. 5 (November 2016): 1002–1026; Stueck, *Korean War*, 120; Shen Zhihua, *Mao, Stalin, and the Korean War* (Abingdon: Routledge, 2012); Thomas Christensen, *Worse Than a Monolith: Alliance Politics and Problems of Coercive Diplomacy in Asia* (Princeton, NJ: Princeton University Press, 2011).

23. Rod Paschall, "Conflict in Korea: Reluctant Dragons and Red Conspiracies," *Military History Quarterly* 12 (Summer 2000): 8–19.

24. Cohen and Gooch, *Military Misfortunes*, 189–90.

25. Stueck, *Korean War*, 125–95; Truman, *Years of Trial and Hope*, 432–50.

26. Cohen and Gooch, *Military Misfortunes*, 194–95; Kissinger, *Diplomacy*, 488–92.

27. Irving Janis, *Victims of Groupthink: A Psychological Study of Foreign Policy and Fiascos* (Boston: Houghton Mifflin, 1972); Acheson, *Present at the Creation*, 466–68, 733; Peter Rodman, *Presidential Command* (New York: Alfred Knopf, 2009), 23.

28. For the U.S. government's internal debate about Taiwan, see David Finkelstein, *From Abandonment to Salvation: Washington's Taiwan Dilemma, 1949–50* (Annapolis, MD: Naval Institute Press, 2014).

29. For a brilliant exposition of the intersection of diplomacy and war, including how the easing of U.S. military pressure prolonged the war in Korea, see Bernard Brodie's *War and Politics* (New York: Macmillan, 1973), 91–104.

30. Acheson, *Present at the Creation*, 466.

Chapter 7

1. For the best of the memoirs of participants, see Henry Kissinger's three volumes. Memoirs of senior Egyptian participants include those by President Anwar Sadat, Foreign Minister Ismail Fahmy, and General Mohamed el-Gamasy. Israeli memoirs include those by Foreign Minister Moshe Dayan and Prime Ministers Golda Meir, Yitzak Rabin, and Shimon Peres. U.S. officials' memoirs include those by Presidents Nixon and Ford. For prewar U.S.

diplomacy, see Yigal Kipnis, *1973: The Road to War* (Charlottesville, VA: Just World, 2013).

2. For Nixon's views in February 1973, see Nina Davis Howland, Craig Daigle, and Edward C. Keefer, *Arab-Israeli Crisis and War, 1973*, Foreign Relations of the United States, 1969–1976, vol. 25, document 25; for Nixon's somewhat fatalistic character, see Henry Kissinger, *Years of Upheaval* (Boston: Little, Brown, 1982).

3. William Quandt, *Peace Process* (Washington, DC: Brookings Institution, 1993), 148–83. Quandt was a senior National Security Council official during the 1970s. For another insightful analysis of Kissinger's diplomacy, see Martin Indyk, *Master of the Game: Henry Kissinger and the Art of Middle East Diplomacy* (New York: Alfred Knopf, 2021). Indyk was the senior NSC official for the Middle East under President Clinton. These are the two best books written by U.S. officials and academics on U.S. policy during and after the 1973 war and postwar negotiations, in addition to Kissinger's own memoirs.

4. Henry Kissinger, *Crisis: The Anatomy of Two Major Foreign Policy Crises* (New York: Simon & Schuster, 2003), passim; see 139–41 for quoted passages. Kissinger's book consists of his declassified meetings and telephone conversations with Nixon and other officials during the war, along with his brief commentary.

5. Kissinger, *Crisis*, 143; Indyk, *Master of the Game*, 123–27.

6. Quandt, *Peace Process*, 153–59.

7. See Indyk, *Master of the Game*, 143–44, for the internal maneuverings among Kissinger, Schlesinger, and Nixon about the resupply to the Israelis.

8. National Security Council staff official William Quandt believes, based on interviews with Israeli military leaders after the war, that the Israelis would have crossed the canal without the airlift but that the airlift may have caused the Israelis to pursue the crossing more aggressively, secure in the knowledge that they had new supplies coming. See Quandt, *Peace Process*, 546–47.

9. Indyk, *Master of the Game*, 174–76.

10. For Soviet archival records on Brezhnev's state of mind, see Sergey Radchenko, "Stumbling toward Armageddon," *New York Times*, October 9, 2018; for overall Soviet policy, see Victor Israelyan, *Inside the Kremlin During the Yom Kippur War* (University Park, PA: Penn State University Press, 1995); Kissinger, *Crisis*, 342.

11. Kissinger, *Crisis*, 370–71.

12. Ibid., 370–412 passim.

13. For the Kissinger postwar negotiations from November 1973 to August 1975, see Kissinger, *Years of Upheaval*, 747–853, 935–78, 1032–1110; Henry Kissinger, *Years of Renewal* (New York: Simon & Schuster, 2000), 347–462; Quandt, *Peace Process*, 183–251; Thomas Parker, *The Road to Camp David: U.S. Negotiating Strategy towards the Arab-Israeli Conflict* (New York: Peter Lang, 1989).

14. Kissinger, *Years of Upheaval*, 615.

15. Ibid., 836.

16. Indyk covers in great detail Kissinger's successful negotiations with Israel and Egypt in November 1973 and January 1974 in *Master of the Game*, 227–338.

17. For the Syrian negotiations, see ibid., 340–409.

18. For the second Sinai negotiations, see ibid., 445–540.

19. Yitzhak Rabin, *The Rabin Memoirs* (Boston: Little, Brown, 1979), 264–65.

20. Author's interview with AIPAC official, January 15, 2015.

Chapter 8

1. Jimmy Carter, *Keeping Faith* (Toronto: Bantam Books, 1983), 19, 21, 23, 142, passim.

2. Zbigniew Brzezinski, *Power and Principle* (New York: Farrar, Straus, Giroux, 1983), 23, 520, 525. Brzezinski wrote one of the most interesting memoirs of a senior U.S. foreign policy official who frequently was at odds with his superior. For an in-depth evaluation of Brzezinski, see Justin Vaïsse, *Zbigniew Brzezinski: America's Grand Strategist*, translated by Catherine Porter (Cambridge, MA: Harvard University Press, 2018).

3. Brzezinski, *Power and Principle*, 432, 520.

4. Carter, *Keeping Faith*, 53–54.

5. For the shah's perceptions about U.S. policy, see Andrew Scott Cooper, *The Fall of Heaven* (London: Macmillan, 2016), passim. For the internal U.S. government differences, see Rodman, *Presidential Command*, 130–36. See also Cyrus Vance, *Hard Choices: Critical Years in America's Foreign Policy* (New York: Simon and Schuster, 1983), 334–48. Vance was not always a major player during deliberations about Iran. His deputy, Warren Christopher, often represented Vance at interagency meetings. Both men wanted the shah to reach out to the opposition, and both men opposed a military crackdown.

6. Brzezinski, *Power and Principle*, 355–56. For Carter's views during 1978–1979, see his *Keeping Faith*, 433–58.

7. On this subject see Mancur Olson, "Rapid Growth as a Destabilizing Force," *Journal of Economic History* 23 (December 1963): 529–52.

8. Interestingly, several years after the shah's fall, Iranian prime minster Bani Sadr would make reference to Brinton's work in a public speech to explain the mayhem that was descending on Iran and that would force Sadr into exile.

9. Brzezinski, *Power and Principle*, 365.

10. Ibid., 371.

11. Ibid., 368.

12. Ibid., 376–81.

13. Ibid., 378.

14. Ibid., 388.

15. Ibid., 477–87. While student radicals took over the U.S. embassy on November 4, seemingly in response to the shah's arrival in the United States, they may have been planning to do so regardless. Student radicals had taken

over the embassy briefly in February 1979, when he was still in Egypt, before being forced to leave the embassy by the Iranian government. The Iranian government still had some independence from Khomeini and his allies, the Revolutionary Guards, at that point.

16. "Why Carter Admitted the Shah," *New York Times Magazine*, May 17, 1981, 36.

17. For these internal debates, see Carter, *Keeping Faith*, 433–58.

18. Cooper, *Fall of Heaven*, 494. Amnesty International did an excellent study of this period.

19. For an excellent account of U.S. government deliberations during this entire period, see Gary Sick, *All Fall Down: America's Tragic Encounter with Iran* (Lincoln, NE: An Author Guild Backinprint.com edition, 2001; originally published 1985 by Random House), 50–151. Gary Sick was the principal White House aide for Iran during the Iranian revolution and hostage crisis. He does not offer a view about whether or not he thought a crackdown would have saved the shah's rule, as Brzezinski forcefully advocated.

Chapter 9

1. See Rodman's *Presidential Command* for an analysis of the effectiveness of George H. W. Bush's foreign policy. President Obama spoke highly of Scowcroft on several occasions.

2. See Colin Powell, *My American Journey* (New York: Random House, 1995), 461; for Scowcroft's view of the war and Bush, see Bartholomew Sparrow, *Brent Scowcroft and the Call of National Security: The Strategist* (New York: Public Affairs, 2015) 421. See also the Scowcroft interview at the presidential oral history project at the Miller Center at the University of Virginia.

3. George Bush and Brent Scowcroft, *A World Transformed* (New York: Vintage, 1999), 317–18.

4. Ibid., 317–24, 354; for the mutual regard and closeness of Bush and Scowcroft, see Sparrow, *Brent Scowcroft*, 425–27; for Powell's explanation for his own dovishness, see Powell, *My American Journey*, 464; for the differences between the army and air force about the prospects for success, see Michael Gordon and General Bernard Trainor, *The Generals' War* (Boston: Little, Brown, 1995), 132. For an overview of the Gulf War, see the study by Scowcroft's Middle East deputy, Richard Haass, *War of Necessity War of Choice: A Memoir of Two Iraq Wars* (New York: Simon & Schuster, 2009).

5. Bush and Scowcroft, *World Transformed*, 325, 329.

6. Ibid., 417.

7. Ibid., 353–54.

8. Powell, *My American Journey*, 488–89.

9. Sparrow, *Brent Scowcroft*, 393; Gordon and Trainor, *Generals' War*, 154.

10. Bush and Scowcroft, *World Transformed*, 283, 385, 432–33.

11. Ibid., 364–65, 409. For Bush's interaction with Gorbachev, see Jeffrey Engel, *When the World Seemed New: George H. W. Bush and the End of the Cold War* (Boston: Mariner, 2018), 376–439.

12. Gordon and Trainor, *Generals' War*, 334–37; Powell, *My American Journey*, 516–17.

13. Powell, *My American Journey*, 523.

14. Bush and Scowcroft, *World Transformed*, 485.

15. For the decision to end the war, see ibid., 520–24; and Bush and Scowcroft, *World Transformed*, 484–85. For the desire for a harder peace among some midlevel Pentagon officials, see Gordon and Trainor, *Generals' War*, 422–26. For the CIA assessment of the destruction of the Republican Guard, see Kenneth Pollack, *The Threatening Storm* (New York: Random House, 2002), 45–46. For the positive impact that the cease-fire had on Saddam's domestic political position, see the account of the former head of Iraqi military intelligence, Wafic al Samarrai, in Oral History: The Iraqis, *Frontline: The Gulf War* (1996), accessed at www.pbs.org/wgbh/pages/frontline/gulf/oral/iraqis.html.

16. Bob Woodward, *The Commanders* (New York: Pocket Books, 1991) 205–206.

17. Robert Gates, *From the Shadows* (New York: Simon & Schuster, 1996) 499.

18. Sparrow, *Brent Scowcroft*, 393.

Chapter 10

1. Robert Gates, *Duty* (New York: Alfred Knopf, 2014), 298.

2. Leon Panetta, *Worthy Fights* (New York: Penguin, 2015), 442–43.

3. Barack Obama, *A Promised Land* (New York: Crown, 2020), 699. Regarding the phrase "stupid stuff," the original statement may have been blunter. The references were widely reported by the press during a presidential trip to Asia in June 2014.

4. Obama subsequently defended the withdrawal by arguing that the Iraqi parliament was not willing to grant a Status of Forces Agreement (SOFA), a standard legal agreement designed to protect U.S. military personnel from arbitrary treatment in foreign courts. Yet the lack of a SOFA did not prevent Obama from sending troops and trainers back to Iraq under a U.S.-Iraqi executive agreement in 2014 to fight the Islamic State.

5. For a revealing account of the administration's internal debates about the Arab Spring, see Gates, *Duty*, 502–10.

6. Ibid., 505.

7. Ibid., 511–23.

8. Ibid., 521.

9. Based on author's discussions with government participants. The author was in the Office of the Secretary of Defense at this time.

10. Gates, *Duty*, 511–23. This failure to anticipate negative results of a policy reminds one of the same mistake made by the Madison administration that declared war on England just when Napoleon's invasion of Russia called for prudence. For an excellent evaluation of the intervention's many negative repercussions, see Alan J. Kuperman, "Obama's Libya Debacle, How a

Well-Meaning Intervention Ended in Failure," *Foreign Affairs* 94, no. 2 (March/April 2015): 66–77.

11. For U.K. decision-making and a critical evaluation of the overall intervention, see the U.K. parliamentary study, House of Commons Foreign Affairs Committee, "Libya: Examination of Intervention and Collapse of the UK's Future Policy Options," Third Report of Session 2016–17 (September 14, 2016).

12. House of Commons Foreign Affairs Committee, "Libya," 13.

13. For the most detailed study on the negative effects of the intervention from a humanitarian viewpoint, see Alan J. Kuperman, "A Model Humanitarian Intervention? Reassessing NATO's Libya Campaign," *International Security* 38, no. 1 (Summer 2013): 105–36.

14. House of Commons Foreign Affairs Committee, "Libya," 18–19.

15. Frederic Wehrey, *The Burning Shores: Inside the Battle for the New Libya* (New York: Farrar, Straus, and Giroux, 2018), 63–64.

16. Robert Gates, "The Overmilitarization of American Foreign Policy," *Foreign Affairs* 99, no. 4 (July/August 2020): 122–25. For Obama's regrets about Libya, see Jeffrey Goldberg, "The Obama Doctrine," *The Atlantic* 317 (April 2016): 70.

17. Mark Mazzetti, Robert Worth, and Michael Gordon, "Obama's Uncertain Path Amid Syria Bloodshed," *New York Times*, October 22, 2013.

18. For the best account of the Syrian red-line incident, see Jeffrey Lewis and Bruno Tertrais, "The Thick Red Line: Implications of the 2013 Chemical Weapons Crisis for Deterrence and Transatlantic Relations," *Survival* 59 (December 2017–January 2018): 77–108.

19. Barack Obama, "Remarks by the President to the White House Press Corps," August 20, 2012, National Archives, https://obamawhitehouse .archives.gov/the-press-office/2012/08/20/remarks-president-white-house -press-corps.

20. Goldberg, "Obama Doctrine," 122–25.

21. Benjamin Barthe, Nathalie Guibert, and Yves-Michel Riols, with Christophe Ayad, "Le choc de l'attaque chimique de la Ghouta, dans la banlieue de Damas," *Le Monde*, February 13, 2014, https://www.lemonde.fr/international /article/2014/02/13/chroniques-syriennes-1-3-a-l-ete-2013-le-choc-de-l-attaque -chimique-en-banlieue-de-damas_4365000_3210.html.

22. Goldberg, "Obama Doctrine," 122–25.

23. Lewis and Tertrais, "The Thick Red Line," 90.

24. John Kerry, "Remarks with United Kingdom Foreign Secretary Hague," September 9, 2013, available at U.S. Department of State, 2009–2017 archive, https://2009-2017.state.gov/secretary/remarks/2013/09/213956.htm.

25. Mark Mazzetti, Robert F. Worth, and Michael R. Gordon, "Obama's Uncertain Path amid Syria Bloodshed," *New York Times*, October 22, 2013.

26. The duplicitous nature of Assad's promise was exposed in the spring of 2017 and 2018 when he killed civilians with chlorine and sarin. President Donald Trump retaliated unilaterally in 2017 and with Britain and France in 2018. Trump did not ask for congressional authorization and received only modest criticism from some congressional Democrats for not doing so. See Helene

Cooper, Thomas Gibbons-Neff, and Ben Hubbard, "U.S., Britain and France Strike Syria over Suspected Chemical Weapons Attack," *New York Times*, April 14, 2018.

27. Goldberg, "Obama Doctrine," 122–25.

28. Ash Carter, *Lessons from a Lifetime of Leadership in the Pentagon: Inside the Five-Sided Box* (New York: Dutton, 2019), 104–105.

29. Goldberg, "Obama Doctrine," 122–25.

Conclusion

1. Chernow, *Alexander Hamilton*, 110.

2. Fred Kaplan, *Lincoln: The Biography of a Writer* (New York: HarperCollins, 2008), 77–78.

3. For more on the issue of electoral reform, see Blake Hounshell and Charles Homans, "With Palin's Defeat, Ranked Choice Voting Vaults into Spotlight," *New York Times*, September 2, 2022; David Montgomery, "How to Save America from Extremism and Authoritarianism by Changing the Way We Vote," *Washington Post Magazine*, November 6, 2022, 13–19; Larry Diamond, "De-Polarizing," *The American Interest* 11, no. 2 (November/December 2015): 41–47.

4. Christian Brose, "The New Revolution in Military Affairs," *Foreign Affairs* 98, no. 3 (May/June 2019): 124.

5. See Fiona S. Cunningham, "The Maritime Rung on the Escalation Ladder: Naval Blockades in a U.S.-China Conflict," *Security Studies* 29, no. 4 (2020): 730–68.

6. Brose, "New Revolution," passim.

7. In 2007 Israel destroyed the Syrian nuclear reactor. During the next decade, the Islamic State took control of that same territory over several years after President Obama withdrew U.S. forces prematurely from Iraq. If the reactor had not been destroyed, the Islamic State might have gained possession of nuclear materials.

8. Drew Miller, "The Age of Designer Plagues," *The American Interest* 12, no. 2 (November/December 2016).

9. For a thoughtful discussion of this issue, see Richard A. Posner, "Torture, Terrorism, and Interrogation," in *Torture: A Collection*, edited by Sanford Levinson (Oxford: Oxford University Press, 2004), 291–98.

INDEX

THOMAS R. PARKER is a professorial lecturer at George Washington University and author of *The Road to Camp David*. He worked for thirty years in diplomatic and military affairs for the White House, U.S. Defense Department, State Department, and the intelligence community.

Printed in the USA
CPSIA information can be obtained
at www.ICGtesting.com
LVHW011916040124
768172LV00005B/35